The Isle of Skye
Mini Guide
by Charles Tait

CONTENTS

Welcome to Skye

Loch nan Eilean, Minginish

THE ISLE OF SKYE is one of the most popular visitor destinations in Scotland and was voted the fourth best island in the world by *National Geographic*. The attraction of the island is well summed up by the noted Sgitheanach, Alexander Robert Forbes, in his *"Place-names of Skye & Adjacent Islands"* (1923):

"Nowhere among the Western Isles is there to be found such a combination of grandness and picturesque originality as in the Isle of Skye. It is past doubt that this island has long since been enthroned as the grandest of them all, the visible queen, whose place and title it would be mere wantonness of disaffection or caprice in any one to dispute."

Portree

The Dramatic Scenery of Skye is mostly due to cataclysmic volcanic eruptions c.65 million years ago (Ma). Beneath the lava flows there are rocks dating back to c.2,800Ma, creating a highly varied landscape. The island is home to c.244 species of breeding birds, as well as c.800 types of wild flowers.

Natural wonders include the jagged Cuillin Ridge, which reaches 993m at Sgurr Alasdair and extends for 7mi (11km). Twelve of the peaks are Munros (peaks over 3,000ft, 914m). The nearby Red Cuillin are more rounded in outline, but just as impressive.

The Old Man of Storr and the Quirang form part of the Trotternish Ridge, another volcanic feature which extends the length of the peninsula. On a much smaller scale, the Fairy Glen and Rha waterfalls offer quite magical experiences.

Coastal Scenery in Skye is equally grand. The majestic cliffs of Duirin-

The
Isle of
Skye
Mini Guide
by Charles Tait

1st Edition

ISBN 9781909036451

The Isle of Skye Mini Guide

1st Edition (2021)
Published by Charles Tait
Kelton, St Ola, Orkney KW15 1TR
Tel 01856 873738
charles.tait@zetnet.co.uk   charles-tait.co.uk

This book is dedicated to Muriel Jane Shearer

Text, design and layout © copyright Charles Tait 2021
Photographs © copyright Charles Tait 1975-2021
Old Photographs from Charles Tait Collection
Printing by J Thomson Colour Printers, Glasgow 202104
Editing & Proofreading by Muriel Jane Shearer
OS maps reproduced from Ordnance Survey mapping with permission
of the Controller of HMSO, © Crown Copyright Reserved 100035677

All rights reserved. No part of this publication may be copied or reproduced in any
form, stored in a retrieval system, or transmitted in any form by any means, elec-
tronic, mechanical, photocopying, recording or otherwise (except for the purpose of
bona fide review) without the prior written permission of the publisher. The author
has asserted his right under the Copyright, Designs and Patents Act 1998 to be
identified as the author of this work.

ISBN 9781909036451

Portree Harbour from Bosville Terrace

ish include Waterstein Head (296m) and Biod an Athair (313m), while Kilt Rock is famous for its Dolerite columns. There are relatively few sandy beaches; these include Talisker Bay, Camusanary, Loch Brittle, Staffin, and the Coral Beaches near Dunvegan.

Visitor Attractions Skye lacks a full scale museum, with the result that there is nowhere to view the story of human settlement on the island, or to get an explanation of its complex geology. The visitor centres at Aros in Portree, Dunvegan Castle, and the Clan Donald Centre are however all excellent. There are several privately run small museums including the Museum of Island Life at Kilmuir. Opening times should be checked before you try to visit, especially outwith the tourist season.

Arts & Crafts The Isle of Skye has a huge range of galleries, workshops and knitwear outlets. These range from established artists and photographers to those just starting out. Skye & Lochalsh Arts & Crafts Association publish an excellent annual "Gallery & Studio Trails Guide".

Accommodation This guide does not include accommodation information, which is found in brochures or online. Skye offers everything from luxurious hotels to hostels. B&Bs are everywhere, as are self catering cottages. There are several campsites.

The Old Man of Storr, Trotternish

Eating Out There is a huge choice of restaurants, cafés, bars and fast food outlets in Skye. These range from the internationally famous Three Chimneys and Kinloch Lodge to several excellent chippies. The many hotels offer menus to suit every wallet and taste, complemented by several wonderfully atmospheric cafés.

Art and Photography The Isle of Skye is an artist's and photographer's dream destination, regardless of the season or weather. The ever changing light, exquisitely dramatic scenery and contrasting terrain make it a hugely popular place to visit.

Cuillin from Elgol

Welcome to Skye

Portree and the Storr from the south

The Aros Experience

Clan Donald Centre

The Skye Bridge from Kyle

Visitor Attractions Skye has a limited number of visitor attractions; these include castles, cultural centres, clan museums, a distillery and a fine modern bridge.

Portree is the main town as well as the administrative and commercial centre. It has a full selection of all types of accommodation, restaurants, cafés, shops and all manner of services. It is clustered above a pretty, sheltered harbour.

Aros on the southern approach to Portree, *"Is a visitor attraction and community cultural centre offering exhibitions, cinema, live music, comedy, dance, drama, theatre, galleries and workshops. With a restaurant, gift shop and children's play areas."*

Clan Donald Centre, at Armadale in southern Sleat, includes the Museum of the Isles, which tells the story of Clan Donald. The restored gardens and woodlands surround the ruins of Armadale Castle. The Armadale Bar and Bistro and two shops have something for everyone. Open from early March to the end of October.

The Skye Bridge was finally opened in 1995, having been rejected as inviable in 1979. Toll free since 2004, it has transformed the economy of Skye; now one of the most popular tourist destinations in Scotland. Those wishing a "true island" experience can still take the ferry from Mallaig to Armadale.

Talisker Distillery, at Carbost on Loch Harport, was established in 1830. Several expressions of its excellent malt whisky can be sampled and purchased at the Visitor Centre. Tours run all year apart from during the silent season, when maintenance takes place. Whilst visiting on no account miss the nearby Oyster Shed.

Talisker Distillery

Flora MacDonald is buried in Kilmuir graveyard, at the north of Trotternish. In 1746 she helped Bonnie Prince Charlie evade the authorities by arranging his passage from South Uist to Skye and onwards. Her memorial is inscribed with a quotation from Samuel Johnson and has a grand view across the Minch to the Outer Hebrides.

Flora MacDonald and Samuel Johnson

Dunvegan Castle and Gardens is situated just north of Dunvegan village. It has been the seat of the MacLeods for over 800 years. As MacLeod of MacLeod says, *"Any visit to the enchanted Isle of Skye must be deemed incomplete without savouring the wealth of history offered by Dunvegan Castle."*

Dunvegan Castle

Broadford from Breakish

Broadford is the second largest settlement on Skye and the first port of call for most visitors. It has a fine setting on a wide bay and has many useful services including a large supermarket, fuel station and interesting shops. With a wide selection of accommodation, restaurants and cafés, it is a good base from which to explore southern Skye.

Welcome to Skye

The Storr and Old Man from the south

The Quiraing from the southwest

Glamaig and the Red Hills

Loch Coruisk

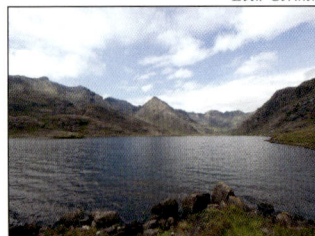

The Old Man of Storr is one of Skye's iconic landmarks. It and its fellow basalt pinnacles are the most prominent part of the 15-mile long Trotternish Ridge, whose east face is one continuous huge landslip. The short, but steep, walk to the Old Man is essential to experience the awe inspiring majesty of nature here. Even better, climb to the top of The Storr.

The Quiraing, just north of Staffin, is one of the most mysterious, dramatic and fantastical places in Britain. Here, a labyrinth of spires, buttresses, and tumbled rocks creates a bizarre and secret world. Much used in science fiction films, the Quiraing is a short walk along an easy path.

The Red Hills dominate the southeast of Skye. These reddish granite hills loom over the landscape from Broadford to Sligachan. Several, including Beinn na Caillach, Glamaig and Marsco are relatively easily climbed. They can also be admired from the roadside reflected in the lochs, at sunset or sunrise, or when covered in snow.

Loch Coruisk lies in the heart of the Cuillin. It is a huge corry scooped out by a glacier and is surrounded by the horseshoe of the Cuillin Ridge. Eleven of these jagged Gabbro peaks are Munros, mountains over 3000ft (914m). Loch Coruisk can be reached from Elgol, from where several operators run regular boat trips.

The Coral Beaches at Claigan, north of Dunvegan, are in fact composed of maerl, not coral. Many regard these sheltered beaches as the best on Skye but they can be crowded on fine days. They are reached by a short signposted walk, but allow plenty of time to relax and fully explore this very different part of Skye. This is also a safe place to swim.

Coral Beaches, Dunvegan

Talisker Bay is perhaps the most romantic of any on Skye. It is approached from Carbost through the dramatic Gleann Oraid with its high cliffs. The bay itself is best at low tide, when a vast area of streaked black and silver sands are exposed, hemmed in by dark cliffs. The mountains of South Uist fill the horizon.

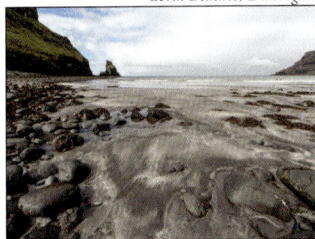

Talisker Bay

The Fairy Pools are in Coire na Creiche at the head of Glen Brittle. This magical cascade of waterfalls, pools and gullies are at their best after heavy rain. In dry weather the flow may stop altogether. They are reached by a short path which may be very muddy and which involves fording streams.

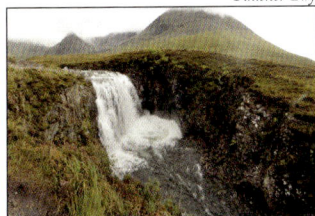

Fairy Pools

Neist Point is the most westerly headland on Skye. This viewpoint is very popular with photographers and is especially impressive at sunset. It is at the end of the B884 from Dunvegan through Duirinish. Along with the cliffs and lighthouse of Neist Point itself, Waterstein Head, Moonen Bay and Loch Mòr all form part of a dramatic and wild landscape.

Neist Point

Welcome to Skye

Kensalayre Standing Stones

Kensalayre, near the head of Loch Snizort at the southwest of Trotternish, has the best standing stones on Skye; the Sornaichean Coir' Fhinn. A third stone is now missing. The giant, Fhinn, roasted deer whole in a huge pot over a fire here. Some of the most impressive and largest Neolithic chambered cairns on Skye stand nearby.

Rubh' an Dùnain

Rubh' an Dùnain is the headland on the south side of Loch Brittle. It is an easy, but quite long, walk from the beach. There is a well-preserved Neolithic chambered cairn, an Iron Age fort, a Viking canal, and ruined tacksman's house all within a small area. Along the way there are particularly fine views over the Cuillin.

Dùn Beag, Bracadale

Dùn Beag is the most accessible well-preserved Iron Age broch on Skye. It stands on a hillock, north of Struan in Bracadale. It is a short walk from a signposted carpark. The broch clearly exhibits all of the main characteristics of these structures. There are fine panoramic views over the Cuillin and Loch Bracadale from here.

Dùn Mór, Bracadale

Dùn Mór is about 500m inland from Dùn Beag, on top of another volcanic hillock. This is probably a Neolithic long cairn, rather than an Iron Age fort. It has well-built terminal wall faces and several chambers. The landscape below it is criss-crossed with ancient field walls and ruinous buildings, all set among lush grass.

Souterrains are underground passages built beneath roundhouses during the Iron Age. There are several in Skye, but the one at Claigan near the Coral Beaches is the easiest to reach and explore. Another, at Kilvaxter in the north of Trotternish, is frequently flooded with water, while most of the rest are in remote areas, or hard to find.

Claigan souterrain

Trumpan Church, in Waternish, witnessed a gruesome event in the vicious internecine clan warfare that went on for centuries. The thatched roof of the church was set alight during a Sunday service in May 1578. Only one woman escaped to raise the alarm. In the ensuing battle nearly all of the attackers were killed.

Trumpan Church, Waternish

Dunscaich Castle, in Sleat, is dramatically sited on an isolated rock. This romantic ruin is the subject of many legends and has a long history of clan feuds, murders, sieges and battles. There are splendid views from here over the Cuillin, Elgol and Blaven. The legendary Cuchillin is said to have built the castle in a day.

Dunscaich Castle, Sleat

Duntulm Castle, Trotternish

Duntulm Castle, at the northern tip of Trotternish, became the MacDonald seat after they abandoned Dunscaich in c.1539. Now a ruin which is slowly collapsing into the sea, this castle was once a splendid fortress which reached its peak in c.1650. The MacDonalds abandoned it in 1732 for their grand new Monkstadt House.

Crown copyright

Kyleakin (G *Caolas Acainn*, Haakon's Narrows - King Haakon's fleet passed through here in 1263) developed as a port during the early 19th century with the building of roads on Skye. There had been a passenger ferry here for hundreds of years. When the Kyle Line opened in 1897 it became the main route into the island.

Since the Skye Bridge opened in 1995 Kyleakin has been much quieter, but is well worth a visit if only for the fine views over the Kyle and the bridge. The village makes a good base from which to explore southern Skye and Lochalsh.

Brightwater Visitor Centre, on the pier, has interactive displays on nature and Skye as well as on Gavin Maxwell, author of *"Ring of Bright Water"*. He lived for a time in the lighthouse cottages on Eilean Bàn, the small island that nestles under the Skye Bridge. There is a nature trail and bird hide. Guided visits to the Maxwell Museum can be booked at the Visitor Centre.

Dùn Aykin (Haakon's Fort), or Caisteal Moil, is a ruined 15th century tower house. It is built on the site of a 10th century Norse castle, said to have belonged to Findanus MacKinnon. His wife

Broadford

Dùn Aykin

The Skye Bridge from Plock of Kyle

was a Norse princess, nicknamed "*Saucy Mary*". They charged a toll for all shipping that wanted to pass through the Kyle. A heavy chain on floats blocked the channel. Mary was buried under an immense cairn on Beinn na Caillich (G Hill of the Old Lady, 732m) above Broadford, from where she can survey her homeland.

Walks There is a short fine walk around South Obbe to Caisteal Moil. The building is now ruinous but has been stabilised to allow safe entry. The nearby hillock, Cnoc a' Fhadhairc (70m), offers excellent panoramic views.

Ashik (ON *Askr Vik*, Ash Tree Bay) is said to be where St Maelrubha first landed on Skye, having crossed from Applecross in the late 7th century. Near the shore, a sacred well, Tobar Ashik (NG688244), is enclosed in a small stone building and fed by a covered lade, or millrace, from a nearby spring. There are still vestiges of an ancient chapel in the adjacent graveyard.

Breakish (ON *Brekka Nis*, Breckness or Slopeness) is the first settlement on the road towards Broadford. There are fine views over Broadford Bay and Beinn na Caillach to the Cuillin from here. Ardnish (G *Aird*, ON *Nis*, Point or Headland) has fine beaches at low tide.

Broadford (ON *Breiðafjorðr*, Broad Firth, population 2011, 747) is the second biggest settlement on Skye. It has a Coop supermarket, filling station, interesting shops, art galleries, a Market Square, restaurants and many places to stay. It is another fine base for exploring southern Skye.

Broadford

KYLEAKIN TO BROADFORD

Beinn na Caillich from Broadford

The Old Pier, which ebbs dry, was built by Telford in c.1809. At this time there were only three houses in Broadford. The completion of the Kyleakin to Portee road in 1812, also by Telford, initiated the rapid development of the village. The modern Gaelic name is *An t-Àth Leathann* (the Ford of the Slope), a mistranslation of the original Old Norse. The second element is *hlið*, a slope, a good example of the frequent mixture of Scottish Gaelic and Old Norse placenames on Skye.

A regular cattle sale was held on the Market Stance (ND674220). In former times the animals were herded to Kyle Rhea and swum across to Glenelg and thence via drove roads to Falkirk or Stir-

Broadford from the Old Pier

ling. When regular steamship services started in 1826 they could instead be shipped south to market.

MacKinnon's, or the Far Pier, *"a commodious little pier a short distance from his mansion"* was built in the 1790s together with fish curing sheds. Nearby Corry Lodge was the seat of the MacKinnons, formerly of nearby Coirechatachan, and is of similar date. It has been described as *"the most elegant of its period in Skye."* The pier remains in use by inshore fishing boats and pleasure craft.

Liveras Chambered Cairn is a large, grassy mound just over the footbridge from the main road. It was partially cleared out in 1832 when the large capstone was removed. It remains at the base of the cairn. A cist inserted in the mound held a Bronze Age beaker.

Arts & Crafts Broadford has a wide range of galleries and interesting small shops. These include jewellery, knitwear, artists' studios, crafts, photography, antiques, and secondhand books. Several are clustered around Skye Market Square and above the Old Pier.

Waterloo is a row of cottages on the east side of Broadford Bay. It was founded for veterans of the Napoleonic Wars. There are beautiful views from here over Broadford and Beinn na Caillich. Ardnish is easy walking with sandy coves and fossils.

Fossils The shores at Breakish, Ardnish and Waterloo have many Jurassic fossils. Gryphaea beds, ammonites, large bivalves and corals are common. Loose stones may be split but do not attempt to break into the underlying rocks. Loose specimens are frequently found after storms. The strata here are from the Lower Jurassic with soft clay shales overlain by hard limestone. The rocks date from the Pliensbachian Period, c.183 to c.191 Ma ago.

KYLERHEA On the east side of Breakish a single track road climbs through Glen Arroch and over Bealach Udal (G Pass of Difficulty, 279m) to Kylerhea. It doubtless got its name due to the problems incurred in driving cattle over the pass.

The Kylerhea ferry *Glenachulish* crosses Caolas an Lamhachaidh (G Sound of Handling at its narrowest point) between Easter and October, . It is the last manually operated turntable ferry in Scotland. A car ferry has run here since 1934 using similar craft.

In former times, thousands of black cattle were swum across this 600m channel at slack water. They were then herded along drove roads to markets in the south. The tide here reaches 8 knots at Spring tides, resulting in eddies and overfalls.

Sgùrr na Coinnich (G Meeting) (NG763223, 739m) overlooks Kylerhea

Kylerhea ferry

and is a steep 2,000m walk from the top of the pass. Just to the north, another Beinn na Cailleach (733m), offers panoramic views over Lochalsh and Kintail.

Otter Haven is a hide next to Kylerhea Minor Light. It is reached by a short trail (1mi, 1.5km) from a signposted carpark. There are public toilets near the carpark. This area is said to be one of the best places in the region to see Otters. Cetaceans, Basking Sharks and White-tailed Eagles may also be spotted.

BEINN NA CAILLICH

(G *Caillich*, Old Woman, 732m) looms over the village. Follow the road signposted "Old Corry" about 1mi (1.5km) north of Broadford to the road end. The summit is a steep scramble 1.25mi (2km) and affords wonderful views in every direction. Thomas Pennant is thought to have been the first visitor to have climbed the mountain, in 1772, when he marvelled at the view of the Blaven and the "Quillin".

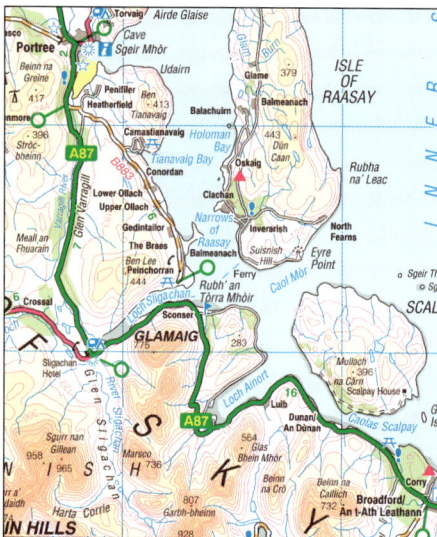

Crown copyright

Storr stand out dramatically against the skyline to the north.

Loch Ainort (ON *Øy Fjorðr*, Island Fiord) is one of the finest sea lochs on Skye and affords stunning views of Glamaig and the Red Hills. This is one of Skye's secrets. When illuminated by a low winter sun on a calm day at high tide, the reflections are perfect. There are several places to stop and admire the view. Care should be taken on this busy road.

BROADFORD TO PORTREE takes about 35 minutes normally on the A87 (25mi, 40km). It can take considerably longer as there are so many spectacular viewpoints to admire along the way. Between Strollamus (ON Strolli's Moss) and Dunan, the Trotternish Ridge and the

Eas a' Bhradain, Loch Ainort

Luib The curved bay of Luib (G bend), on the south shore of Loch Ainort has a renovated blackhouse complete with a thatched roof. There are several interesting nousts above the shore where boats were hauled out. The views over Loch Ainort are spectacular from here.

Walk to Torrin (11mi, 18km) From Luib there is a fine low level walk to Torrin on Loch Slapin. The route follows Srath Mhor southwards for 4mi (6km), passing Clach Oscar before reaching Torrin. The Blue Shed Café is an excellent half way point. Return by the same route or follow a path north via Strath Beag to the old road above Strollamus.

The Red Hills from Loch Ainort

The route should not be attempted after heavy rain as the streams will be in spate.

Eas a' Bhradain (G Waterfall of Salmon, NG534266), at the head of Loch Ainort, can be spectacular after heavy rain. Park in the adjacent layby, taking care crossing this busy road. The best views require traversing very wet ground to reach the river. There is another layby about 1,000m further on, also with good views.

Moll (ON *Mol*, Shingle Beach) The old road north to Sligachan follows the coast of Moll for c.5mi (8km). It is signposted at the head of Loch Ainort and just south of Sconser golf course. Although badly maintained and single track, this very scenic route offers unique views of Loch Ainort, Scalpay and Raasay as well as fish farms and quarries.

Glamaig (G Greedy Woman, 775m) dominates the A87 from Loch Ainort to north of Sligachan. Several laybys have fine panoramas over the hill and its neighbours Beinn Dearg Mhór (G

Dearg, Red, 731m) and Marsco (736m). All can be climbed from the head of Loch Ainort but the established routes start at Sligachan or near Sconser.

Sconser is the terminal for the Raasay ferry, a modern diesel electric hybrid vessel. It is also home to the 9-hole Isle of Skye Golf Course, one of only two on the island. Sconser is famous for being the birthplace of John MacKenzie (1856–1933), said to have first climbed Sgur na Gillean as a boy. Sgurr Mhic Choinnich (G Mackenzie's Peak) is named in his honour.

Sligachan (G *Sligeach*, Shelly Place) has been the gateway to the Cuillin since the

Glamaig from Sligachan

Broadford to Portree

Glamaig and Beinn Dearg Mhór from Sligachan

present hotel was opened in the 1830s. Generations of climbers and many famous people have been guests here. Sir Harry Lauder, the music hall comedian, singer and character (1870-1950) in the visitors' book, *"The hills are bare & bonnie, the road is lang & steep, But the air is soft & balmy, Skye's the place to sleep!"*

The A87 continues northwards to Portree (10mi, 16km), while the A863 follows the west coast to Dunvegan (24mi, 38km). With its location, unique views of the Cuillin, hotel, restaurant, and campsite, Sligachan makes a good base.

Varragill (ON *Varda Gill*, Watch Ravine) The A87 follows the Varragill River

Portree from Penifiler

to Loch Portree. Increasingly spectacular views over Portree and The Storr unfold along the way. Varragill was once well populated, with a substantial settlement near where the Varragill Burn joins the river. (NG475377). There are field walls, lazy beds and the remains of at least 12 substantial houses.

The road is lined with Forest Enterprise conifer plantations; some have been harvested but not replanted. South of Portree, the scene has little changed since William Daniell's aquatint of 1815. The bridge remains narrow, but there are many more houses and trees.

Inveralivaig (G *inver*, river mouth; ON *Olaf's Vik*, Olaf's Bay) is the last of several small settlements on the east side of Loch Portree. It can be reached by a track from Penifiler (G *Peihinn an Fhidhleir*, Fiddler's Pennyland).

The tidal islet of Eilean Chalium-cille has an ancient chapel, said to be dedicated to St Columba. Loch Portree was formerly known as Loch Chalium Cille. The nearby small sandy beach of

Camas Bàn is both secluded and sheltered. Please park with care and do not obstruct access roads or gates.

Braes The single track B883 crosses moorland to the east coast from Peinmore. It reaches the east coast at Camastianavaig with its pretty little beach (ON *Dyn Vik*, Noisy Bay?). This is a perfect picnic spot, with fine views over Raasay Sound.

Fossils A trail goes northwards from the carpark to a small headland (NG520532). Early Jurassic sediments here have belemnites, bivalves and ammonites. Fossils should only be sought on the foreshore among loose rocks. The cliffs should not be approached. There may be restricted access during the breeding season as White-tailed Sea Eagles nest on the cliffs north of here.

The road continues south through a series of small settlements with interesting names. These include Achnahanaid, Ollach, Gedintailor, and Balmeanach, as well as Braes itself (NG517365). At the end of the road, Peinachorrain faces the northeast entrance to Loch Sligachan.

Walk The old road from Sligachan to Portree ran along the shore below the steep slopes of An Leitir, then via Braes. It was

Battle of the Braes memorial

abandoned after the Glen Varragill road was built in the early 1800s. Today it is a tranquil 7mi (11km) lochside scenic route with excellent views. Towards the Sligachan end the terrain gets boggy and there are several streams to cross, so this route is not recommended after heavy rain.

Camas a' Mhór Bheòil (G Widemouthed Bay) is a beautiful little beach of pebbles and sand near the end of the road below Braes. It is sheltered from all directions except the north and enclosed by a small peninsula. With a ruined dùn, Dùnan an Aisilidh, a lochan, small caves, and a natural arch this is a fine place for quiet exploration.

Camas a' Mhór Bheòil

SLEAT PENINSULA

Crown Copyright

Armadale is sign-posted off the A87 at Skulamus. The A851 is now full width for the entire 16mi (25km). The ferry from Armadale to Mallaig runs all year and takes about 30 minutes to cross the Sound of Sleat. This route saves consider-able driving time when approaching from the south.

The Black Lochs For the first few miles the route passes through bleak heather moor-land. This extends down the spine of Sleat due to underlying Tor-ridonian Sandstone. The Black Lochs near Drochaid Airigh na Saorach (G Bridge of the Shieling of Labour) can appear either foreboding or strikingly beautiful, depending on the light. A water-horse, or Kelpie (G *Each-Uisge*), is said to inhabit these lochs.

SLEAT (ON *Slettr*, Smooth, Sleek, Flat) is called *"The Garden of Skye"* because of its lush, green vegetation, especially on the southeast coast.

Kinloch (G *Cean*, Head of the Loch) has a large Forest Enterprise conifer plantation. The head of Loch na Dal is a small estuary with a salt marsh. In season it is awash with

Isle Ornsay Pier

the mauve of Sea Pinks and later, Sea Aster. Otters may be seen here.

Kinloch Lodge Hotel was cited in the Conde Naste Traveller magazine as one of the world's top 25 small hotels. Lady Claire MacDonald is married to Lord Macdonald, Chief of Clan Donald. *"For near four decades, the Macdonalds have run their Isle of Skye home, Kinloch Lodge, as a unique luxury hotel with blazing log fires and ancestral portraits."*

Isle Ornsay

Lady Claire is also famous for her best-selling cookery books. *"She is also admired for a remarkable willingness to share the secrets of her kitchen, and celebrated for her truly wonderful sense of fun. All of this comes together splendidly in the three-day residential cookery courses Claire hosts at Kinloch Lodge."*

Isle Ornsay (ON *Fjara-ey*, Ebb Tide Island) is named after the tidal island which shelters its pretty little harbour. Also known as Eilean Iarmain (Dhiarmaid's Isle), this pretty little village of white-washed houses dates from the early 1800s, when the pier was built.

For a time this was a busy Herring port. From 1826, steamships called here and it became one of Skye's first holiday destinations. With its romantic old inn, The Eilean Iarmain Hotel, Gallery An Talla Dearg, Floaidh boutique, and exquisite little harbour, Isle Ornsay has much to offer the visitor.

Pràban na Linne (G The Gaelic Whiskies) was established by Sir Iain Noble in 1976 *"to provide authentic whisky for the Gaelic speaking islands..... our whiskies are not chill filtered. This ensures that the whiskies are of unequalled quality and historical authenticity."* The company

Isle Ornsay lighthouse

Sleat Peninsula

The Cuillin from Ord

produces three whiskies, *Poit Dhubh, Te Bheag and Mac Na Mara*. The first is a malt, the others are fine blends. All are claimed as *"Real Whisky as it used to be."*

Loch an Dubrachan has for long been said to have harboured a water-horse (G *Each-Uisge*). At times it would take the form of a hansome young man who would woo the local girls, but then carry them off to their deaths. People became so worried that MacDonald ordered that the loch be swept from end to end with nets, but nothing was found.

The West Loop Road crosses the moor from just south of Loch nan Dubrachan

The Black Lochs

to the west coast at Ord. This very pretty route then twists and turns along the coast through Tokavaig and Tarskavaig before returning to the east coast at Ostaig. This fertile area is lush and green due to being on a large outcrop of Cambrian Durness Limestone.

Ancient Woodlands The west side of Sleat has several areas of ancient woodland with Oak, Ash, Alder, Hazel, and Silver Birch. Lichens, mosses, and liverworts not seen elsewhere are a particular feature. The most accessible are on the road from Ord to Tokavaig and in Coille a' Glasgain, east of Ord.

Loch Eishort (ON *Iss Fjordr*, Ice Fiord) separates the remote and deserted headland of Suisinish from Sleat. The remote and uninhabited south coast between Ord and Drumfearn also has several areas of relict woodland. Much of this is in sheltered valleys,

Tarksavaig

where sheep and deer cannot reach. Ord is the best place from which to explore this lonely coast.

Ord (G *Aird*, Headland) is situated on a steep slope on the north bank of the Ord River. The dramatic view over the Cuillin is one of the best in Skye. Teampuill Chaon, dedicated to St Congan or Choan, is an ancient ruined chapel. It is surrounded by an interesting graveyard with many very old marker stones. On the shore nearby, Tobar Chaon is one of several holy wells here.

Tokavaig (ON *Orkn Vagr*, Seal Bay) with its pretty bay, ancient woodlands, and stunning views, is a place to savour, summer sunsets over the Cuillin are spectacular. Dunsciach Castle is on a large rock, joined to the nearby headland by a bridge and stairway. The whole area beyond must have been an impressive series of buildings.

DUNSCAICH CASTLE

This ancient castle (G *The Fort of Doom*) is dramatically situated on an isolated rock off the northwest point of Tokavaig, or Ob Gauscavaig. Many legends are told about Cuchullin and his supporters who arrived here from Ulster, and built the castle in a day.

This excellent site may well have had a vitrified Iron Age Fort and then a Norse one long before the present castle was built, in around 1266.

Dunscaich was occupied by MacLeods, MacKaskills, and the MacDonalds, from 1449 when they gained the title to Sleat. The castle had a long history of clan feuds. Murders, battles, sieges, vendettas, and many dreadful deeds, some true, other legends, happened here. The MacDonalds abandoned Dunscaich for Duntulm in Trotternish in c.1539.

Tarskavaig (ON *Þorskr Vagr*, Cod Bay) was a fishing station until the 20th century. Cod and Lythe were caught with

Dunscaich Castle

Sleat Peninsula

Armadale

longlines in the nearby waters, especially on the Seagull Bank. In former times the fish were salted and dried but after the Mallaig railway opened in 1901 they were landed there fresh. Larger boats made this type of fishing inviable.

Viewpoint The road back across the moor to Ostaig passes the dark and mysterious Loch Dhughall. A little further on, there is a fine view down Glean Meadhonach to Loch a' Ghille. Above Inver Dalavil the sad ruins of a cleared village overlook a ditch. This was dug in

a failed attempt to drain the loch. There are small areas of ancient woodland surviving here in sheltered ravines.

Castle Camus or Knock Castle (G *Cnoc, Hillock*) overlooks its pretty bay and the township of Teangue. This fine defensive position probably had an Iron Age broch, and perhaps a Norse keep, before the present tower house was built around 1300. The castle was an important MacDonald stronghold for many years, but by 1690 it was abandoned.

Castle Camus or Knock Castle

Sabhal Mòr Ostaig (ON *Austr Vagr*, East Bay) was founded by financier Sir Ian Noble in 1973. He bought the Eilean Iarmain Estate in 1972 after being inspired by the revival of the Faroese language. His vision was to create a Gaelic linguistic and cultural renaissance. The main goal of increasing access to and learning of Gaelic has been achieved.

Armadale has a year round car ferry to Mallaig, across the Sound of Sleat. Regular steamer services stopped here from c.1826. They ran from Mallaig after the railway opened in 1901. There are several interesting shops and galleries. The Clan Donald Centre, at Armadale Castle, has an interesting museum and woodland walks.

Ardvasar, the biggest settlement in Sleat, was home to Isle of Skye Yachts, now closed. Moorings are available here. The village is a good base from which to explore the peninsula. The hotel is one of the oldest on Skye. It dates from the building of the Parliamentary Road from here to Broadford, in 1812.

Aird of Sleat is 5mi (8km) south of Armadale along a twisting single track lane, mostly lined with woodland. At the end of the road there are panoramic views across the Sound of Sleat as well as to Rum, Eigg and Canna. A ruined broch, Dùn Bàn sits above the shore (NG599005). This is the most southerly of a line of at least seven such sites between here and Isle Ornsay.

Point of Sleat is about 2.5mi (4km) from the end of the public road

> ### CLAN DONALD CENTRE
>
> The Clan Donald Lands Trust purchased the 8,000ha estate in southern Sleat in 1971. Today Clan Donald Skye is a major visitor attraction with restored gardens. There is 16ha of mature woodland with a large variety of trees, some 200 years old, around Armadale Castle.
>
> The Museum of the Isles tells the story of Clan Donald in six galleries, with a Library and Study Centre. The ruins of Armadale Castle have been consolidated and landscaped.
>
> With the Stables Cafe, Gatehouse, and Museum Shops there is something for everyone. The Centre is open daily from the end of March to the end of October. The gardens may be visited out of season.

(NG589008) along a rough track. A secret sandy beach, Camas Daraich, nestles in a small secluded cove to the east of the lighthouse.

Aird of Sleat

Loch Coruisk is surrounded by the Cuillin Ridge

STRATHAIRD & ELGOL - SRATH NA H-ÀIRDE

Crown copyright

STRATHAIRD (G *Aird an t-Srath*, Headland of the Valley) historically stretched from Broadford to Elgol and was held by the MacKinnons of Coirechatachan. Most of this area is composed of Cambrian Limestone and Jurassic sediments, making it generally fertile. The John Muir Trust bought the 2,020ha Torrin estate in 1991. Three years later it acquired the 6,000ha Strathaird Estate.

Strath Suardal (ON *Svordr Dalr*, Sward Dale) is named for its lush pastures. It supported a substantial population for thousands of years until almost the whole area was cleared of people in the mid-19th century. Many species of limestone-loving wild flowers thrive here, including at least 12 types of orchids.

Volcanic Vent Between Cill Chriosd and Kilbride, on the lower slopes of Beinn Dearg Bheag, the vent of a major volcano can be seen. This large feature is about 3mi (4.5km) across. It is filled with coarse pyroclastic rocks associated with an explosive eruption. Large pieces of limestone, sandstone, and basalt are intermingled with volcanic rocks.

An Sithean (NG62720, 33m) is a grassy fairy mound which overlooks the valley from a sharp bend in the road. At full moon fairies are said to be seen dancing around the stones here. Their evocative and enchanting music may also be heard, but only by a few!

A more prosaic explanation is that the mound is the remains of a Neolithic

An Sithean, Suardal

Suardal from Torrin

chambered cairn. The standing stone is a remaining upright orthostat. To the east, several rings of stones represent the foundations of Bronze Age houses.

From here a track goes northwest to a ford. The remains of Coirechatachan House, where the MacKinnons entertained Johnson and Boswell in 1773, stand in a picturesque spot overlooking Suardal.

Loch Cill Chroisd with Beinn Mhòr Dearg and Beinn na Caillich

Cill Chriosd (G Church of Christ) probably dates from the 16th century, but was undoubtedly built in place of a much older chapel. It is surrounded by an ancient graveyard with many very old grave markers. A small mausoleum has many MacKinnon memorials, while there are several interesting carved stones.

Loch Cill Chriosd was home to a water-horse (G *Each-Uisge*) which wreaked havoc in the neighbourhood, until St Maelrubha exorcised it by blessing the waters. In another story it was St Columba himself who asked for divine intervention, thus transforming the evil spirits in the water, making them virtuous. Either way, the water-horse never again made off with young ladies.

Birds Reed Warblers and Little Grebe breed here. Herons may be seen stalking fish, while in summer the loch has many White and Yellow Water Lilies on its surface. In early autumn many Swallows congregate at the loch prior to migration; feeding on flies and roosting in the reeds. In winter, Goldeneye, Tufted Duck, other migrating waterfowl, and Whooper Swans are present.

Cill na Chroisd

Loch Slapin from Suisinish track

Torrin from Blaven

Wild Flowers Mountain Avens is common on limestone in Suardal, Torrin and at Camas Malag. Dark-red Helleborine, Lesser and Common Twayblades, Fragrant, Lesser Butterfly and Frog Orchids may also be found. Where limestone is exposed, the small cliffs, grikes, and clints support a wide range of grasses, ferns, and wild flowers.

Kilbride The scant remains of a chapel dedicated to St Bride lie above the road just before Torrin. On the other side Clach na h'Annait stone and the nearby Tobar na'h'Annait well are mysterious names from the distant past. They may be pre-Christian sites taken over by an early saint, perhaps part of a Neolithic stone circle and religious centre. The Oystercatcher is named after St Bride in Gaelic, *Gille-brighde*.

Torrin (G Mound) is a pretty little township with lush fields of grass, beautiful wild flowers and the dramatic backdrop of Blaven. The Blue Shed Café has a stunning view together with excellent food and service. It is well worth a stop if it is open. It is closed out of season.

Torrin Marble formed when Cambrian limestone was metamorphosed by heat from a nearby magma chamber. This hard, magnesium rich rock has been used for agricultural dressing, building materials, and decorative finishings.

Today this is the only marble quarry in the UK. Operated by the Leith Group, it produces large quantities of aggregate for the building trade. Skye marble is also used to make jewellery and souvenirs.

Camas Malag is reached by a narrow lane which branches off the B8083 just before Kilbride

Blaven from Torrin

(NG582193). This pebble beach has granite, limestone, marble, Jurassic, and dolerite outcrops, and has stunning views over Loch Slapin and Blaven.

High Pastures Cave (G *Uamh An Ard Achadh*) is off the road to Camas Malag (NG594197).

Camas Malag, Loch Slapin

The limestone cave system here extends to at least 320m, one of the longest on Skye. There are many other caves in this area; none should be entered without specialist knowledge and equipment. High Pastures Cave has been extensively excavated; finds date from the late Bronze Age and early Iron Age.

Suisinish house with Rowan trees

Torrin Marble Quarry

Suisinish & Boreraig

These deserted villages were cleared in 1853 and 1854 by Lord MacDonald to make more money by letting the land as a sheep ranch. A fine walk from Camas Malag follows a Land Rover track and paths, c.10mi (16km).

The houses were set on fire to prevent the inhabitants from returning. This fertile area has standing stones, hut circles, and field walls. A ruined broch at Boreraig is testimony to the longevity of this destroyed community.

From Boreraig, go north across the moor, passing the Beinn nan Carn Native Woodland. Over 200,000 trees were planted in an enclosure to exclude sheep and deer. Return past an old marble quarry to Loch Cill Chriosd and thence the public road.

This sad peninsula is made more poignant by the comments of geologist Archibald Geikie, *"A cry of grief went up to heaven, a long plaintive wail"*.

Panoramic view over the Cuillin and Glen Sligachan from Blaven

BLAVEN (ON *Blá Fjall*, Blue Mountain, 928m) is reckoned by many to be among the finest in the Highlands. It is separated from the rest of the Cuillin by the precipitous glacial valley of Srath na Créitheach. Together with Garbh Beinn (806m) to the north, it forms a very daunting outlier of the main Cuillin Ridge. The views across Loch Slapin from Torrin are particularly impressive.

Blaven is composed mostly of Gabbro. Cataclysmic volcanic events took place here c.65Ma in close proximity to Cambrian limestone, Jurassic sediments and granites. The result is mixed exposures of all these rocks, especially on the south facing parts of the mountain.

Coire Uaigneach (G Secret or Remote Corry) is by every definition a special place for those interested in botany. Jurassic limestones outcrop on the cliffs here where a profusion of lime-loving plants thrive. These include Roseroot, Alpine Lady's Mantle, Globeflower, Alpine Saw-wort, and Alpine Meadow-Rue. Large banks of Purple and Yellow Saxifrage are resplendent in early spring and summer respectively.

Summit Panorama The views from the top of Blaven are unique. This is the only position from where the Cuillin Ridge can be observed from its own altitude. To the left, Glen Sligachan curves down past Marsco and Glamaig to the

Allt na Dinaiche, Blaven

Coire Uaigneith, Blaven

sea. To the east, Garbh Beinn looms above Beinn na Caillich, while to the south are Camasunary and Elgol.

Keppoch (G *a Cheapach*, Cultivated Area) is 2mi (3.5km) south of the Blaven carpark. This was a thriving settlement of 44 families until it was cleared for sheep in 1852. In more recent times, the John Muir Trust has felled the conifers planted over the village by the Forestry Commission. A footpath leads through the woods. The site can also be reached from the public road (NG182557).

Clach Oscar (NG563226) is a large broken rock about 300m from the head of Loch Slapin. In legend it was tossed here by Oscar, a giant in the time of Fingal. Before the coast road from Broadford to Portree was built, the route from Sligachan to Portree went via Srath Mor to Luib. The boulders are host to a lichen, *Lasallia pustulata*, or Rock Tripe.

Loch Slapin and Torrin from Blaven

BLAVEN

Blaven (928m, 3,044ft) is one of twelve Munros, mountains over 3,000ft (914.4m), on Skye. Unlike the other Cuillin its summit can be reached by any fit walker and does not involve venturing into remote areas. The panoramic views of the Cuillin Ridge, Red Hills and beyond are quite simply stupendous.

Popular Route From the carpark next to Allt Dunaiche (NG561217) follow a clear path past streams and waterfalls to Coire Uaigneach with its steep cliffs. From the top of Fionna-Choire, turn right and follow cairns to the summit. Descend by the same route, taking care to follow the cairns (5mi, 8km).

Blaven should only be attempted during clear, fine weather and never after heavy rain when the streams may become torrents.

Clach Oscar

Strathaird & Elgol - Srath na h-Àirde

Loch Slapin from west of Torrin

Loch Slapin (G *laban*, myre) is a long, shallow sea loch with a muddy bottom. At its head there are large areas of salt marsh. The road may be flooded at very high tides. Several viewpoints afford dramatic panoramas of the mountains.

Kilmarie (G Church of St Maolrubha) has an ancient graveyard with Yew and Cypress trees. The church and a stone circle were washed away in a storm. The cemetery has many old gravemarkers.

Chambered Cairn *Cnocan nan Gobhar* (G Goat's Knowe, NG553173) is over a footbridge from the graveyard. It was partially excavated in the 1920s, when a Bronze Age grave containing a Beak-

er-style urn was found inserted near the top of the cairn. The stone cist can still be seen. This is one of the best preserved Neolithic chambered cairns on Skye. It measures 22x17.5m and is 4.5m high. No entrance passage is visible.

Dùn Ringill (ON *Rinn Gill*, Promontory Ravine, NG562171) is an Iron Age broch, c.800m east of the cairn, along a path through woods and along the coast. Unlike many brochs, Dùn Ringill continued in use until recent times. It was the residence of the MacKinnons, before they removed to Castle Moil. The building is 4m high and surrounded by a deep ditch. The entrance passage is intact, while the ruins of several substan-

Kilmarie

Dùn Rinigill

Camasunary from An Nam, Sgurr na Stri in background

tial buildings of unknown age lie nearby. Two boat slipways lead to the shore.

Camusanary (G *Camas Fhionn Airidh*, Bay of the Fair Shieling) is a beautiful and remote sandy bay facing Loch Scavaig. A coastal path goes south to Elgol, while the rugged Sgurr na Stri rears to the west. Inland, the south ridge and summit of Blaven dominate the view. Although only a short distance from the main road, Camasunary has a delightfully remote feeling. It is popular as a base for hikers and climbers.

Bothy A new bothy was completed at Camasunary in 2014 by 59 Commando Squadron Royal Engineers, for the Mountain Bothy Association.

Walks All of the walks described here offer outstanding views of the Cuillin and Loch Slapin.

Camasunary

Camasunary is one of the finest beaches in Skye. It can be reached by several routes, either directly or as part of a longer, more strenuous hike.

Kilmarie Route From the signposted carpark, just south of Kilmarie (NDG545173) follow a rough track over the bealach of An Nam, and then down to a narrow bridge over a burn to reach the beach, 2.5mi (4km).

Camasunary is a beautiful sandy beach

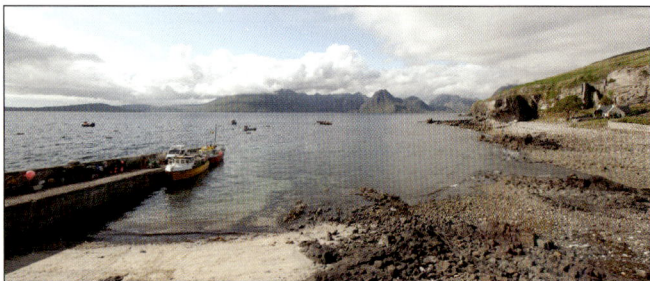

Elgol jetty and beach with Loch Scavaig and the Cuillin

ELGOL (ON *Helga Bolstaðir*, Holy Farm) lies in a fertile little valley facing the Cuillin and Loch Scavaig in what must be one of the most enchanting locations of any township. The view is claimed to be the best in all of Scotland. The land here is fertile, making it attractive for early settlers. There is a fine, sheltered beach for pulling up boats; the adjacent sea has excellent fishing grounds.

Fossils The Elgol Sandstone and Lealt Shale formations date from the Middle Jurassic, c.170Ma. The most interesting fossils here are clams of the *Cyrenia* family which can be found in sandstone pebbles on the shore to the north of the bay and around the headland.

Elgol boat trips

Boat Trips Depending on the weather, boat trips are operated year round from Elgol jetty to Loch Coruisk, . Wildlife watching excursions as well as visits to Rum, Canna and Soay are available in the tourist season. Booking is essential.

Dùn Grugaig (G Sulky Woman's Fort, NG535123) is a massive stone structure built across a small headland. The wall is over 4m thick and stands nearly 4.5m high. The entrance, complete with its huge lintel, remains intact. Scattered stones are all that remains of its internal structures.

Spar Cave (NG537130) is so named on account of the spectacular limestone formations which have formed within it. Despite Victorian visitors having broken off the best ones, this cave is well worth a visit. G *Uamh Altruimin*, Cave of Nursing, so called because of a legendary young lady who fell pregnant to her lover from Colonsay, and was hidden here from her vengeful father.

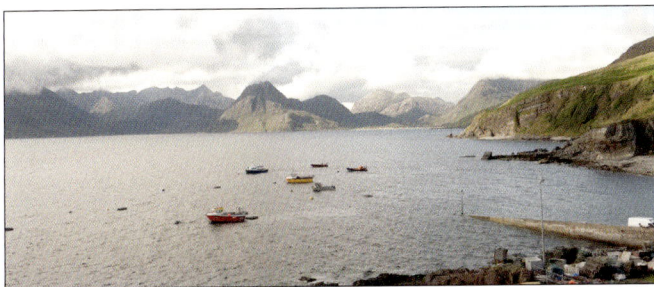

Elgol jetty and beach with Loch Scavaig and the Cuillin

Access to the shore is by a steep path which starts 200m south of the Glasnacille phonebox. Spar Cave is about 200m north at the head of a vertically sided geo. The interior of the cave is completely covered in *Spar*; limestone which has crystallised in curious formations. After climbing a steep "stairway", the cave levels out, before ending at a small pool.

The cave can only be accessed at low water by clambering over very slippery rocks. The best plan is to reach the shore about 2 hours before low tide, thus allowing plenty of time to visit the cave and return. A torch is essential.

Prince Charlie's Cave (NG516123) is c.1mi (1.5km) south of Elgol, on the west side of a small bay, Port an Luig Mhoir. A path follows the coast southwards along the cliffs. Here the fugitive was hidden by the MacKinnons prior to being taken to Mallaig. The cave can only be accessed at low tide.

Suidhe Biorach (G Sharp Seat) overlooks the cave. It is believed that childless ladies may be able to conceive after sitting here. Whether there is any truth in the story is unknown, but the view is indeed very peaceful and romantic.

Elgol limestone beach

Elgol eroded limestone

Loch Coruisk

LOCH CORUISK (G *Coire Uisg*, Corry of the Water) was formed by glaciers. Its depth is said to reach 38m below sea level in places. Depending on the season, time of day, and light, the waters can be black and forbidding, or bright blue and sparkling. On calm days the Cuillin are reflected, while in stormy weather the place takes on a menacing aura.

The best time to visit is on a calm summer morning when the sun shines down the loch and lights up every feature. Because of the height of the mountains and the narrowness of the valley, such periods are transient. Most of the time the southwest side is in shadow. Alternatively a calm, sunny winter's day with snow on the tops is hard to beat.

Visitors' Comments Sir Walter Scott described it as a *"stern, dread lake"*, while MacCulloch wrote in 1883 that, *"It is not surprising that Coruisk should be considered by the natives as the haunt of the water-goblin or of spirits still more dreadful."* There are no records of young ladies, or indeed any other visitors *"falling into the fangs of the kelpie."*

Coruisk Memorial Hut is about 100m from the landing. It is an ideal base

The Cuillin from Elgol

Loch Scavaig and the Cuillin by Daniell

from which to explore the surrounding area for a couple of days rather than be rushed between boat schedules. The hut is run by the Junior Mountaineering Club of Scotland. Campers may use the facilities for a small fee.

Sgùrr na Stri (G Hill of Strife, 494m) is an eastern outlier of the Cuillin. This hill and its northern extension, Sgurr Hain, are separated from the main ridge by Coire Riabhach, and from Blaven by the deep Srath na Creitheach. Despite its small size, the summit of Sgurr na Stri is ideally situated to give one of the best views in Scotland.

From here, the whole Cuillin Ridge forms a horseshoe around Loch Coruisk. The views over Blaven, Elgol, and the islands to the south are also very impressive. For maximum benefit Sgùrr na Stri needs a fine clear day. Summer sunsets are especially dramatic from here. Another good time to come is when the high tops have a dusting of snow. Either require advance planning.

Loch Coruisk

Boat Trips Several operators offer boat trips from Elgol to Loch Coruisk.

Circular Walk Cross the river at the stepping stones and bear left around the loch, crossing a stream just before a pebble beach. The path continues along the northeast shore of the loch with ever more spectacular views of the peaks.

At the loch head continue into Coir'-uisg in the centre of the Cuillin. From here In Pinn (the Inaccessible Pinnacle) stands out on Sgùrr Dearg (986m) to the west. Return via the southwest side keeping to the shore or just above the boggy areas on the bare gabbro rocks, 5mi, 8km, 4 hours.

Air Crash In December 1982 a US Airforce F111F crashed on Sgùrr na Stri with the tragic loss of both crew, who had no time to eject. A memorial plaque at Elgol commemorates the unfortunate young men who died on that wild December night.

Sgurr na Stri and Camasunary

Sligachan Bridge with the river in spate after heavy rain

MINGINISH & CUILLIN - MINGINIS

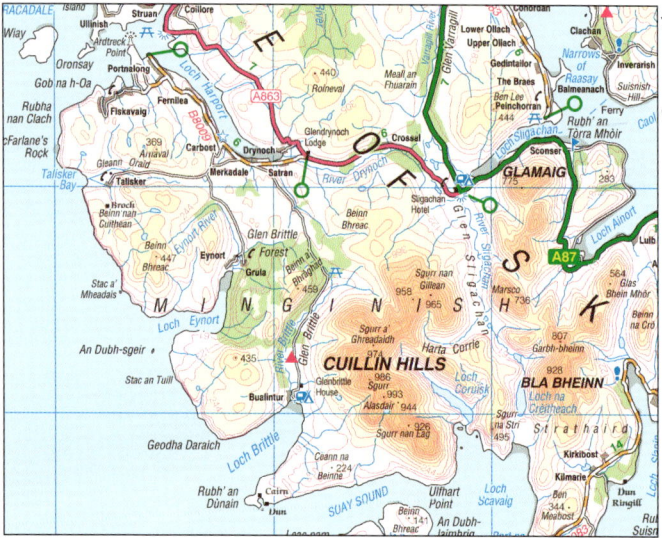

Crown copyright

MINGINISH (ON *Mikil Nes*, Great Headland) includes the Cuillin, the Red Hills, and the peninsula south of Loch Harport to the west. Geologically the whole area is volcanic in origin with pink granite, black gabbro, basalt, and dolerite defining the landscape.

Sligachan (G *Sligeach*, Shelly Place) is the gateway to Minginish and the northern parts of Skye. From here the A87 continues northwards to Portree (10mi, 16km), while the A863 follows the west coast to Drynoch (9mi, 15km) and the western side of Minginish. Sligachan is a good base for exploring this area.

Sligachan River in spate with Cuillin in background

The **Cuillin** dominate the views from Sligachan. To the south-west the jagged peaks of Am Bàsteir and Sgùrr na Gillean mark the north-eastern end of the Cuillin Ridge. The old bridge over the Sligachan River was built by Thomas Telford in c.1812. It was replaced by a modern structure which provides one of Skye's most photographed views.

Glamaig and the Red Hills from Sligachan

The Red Hills lie to the east and south. Their pink granite has eroded to much more rounded contours, covered in places with vast areas of scree. Glamaig looms over the landscape, looking conical from this angle. Behind, Beinn Dearg Mhòr, Beinn Dearg Mheadhonach, and Marsco march in a line along the deep glaciated Glen Sligachan.

Glen Sligachan was an important route from the north to the south of Skye. It was used by both the MacDonalds and the MacLeods during their centuries of raiding, cattle stealing, and clan warfare.

The Battle of Sligachan was fought between these two clans in 1395. On this occasion the MacDonalds were chased back to Eynort, where they had landed. Unable to reach their galleys, they were slaughtered and their severed heads displayed at Dunvegan Castle.

The Cuillin from Sligachan

The Red Hills from Glen Drynoch

Loch nan Eilean and snow on Cuillin

Marsco and Sgurr nan Gillean from the A863

Harta Corry A famous battle was fought in Harta Corry between these two clans. There was great loss of life, including all of the MacLeods present. Bodies were piled up high around the Bloody Stone (NG488237), or the Rock of the Flaying, a huge glacial erratic boulder.

Loch nan Eilean

Loch nan Eilean (NG472306) on the A863 just northwest of Sligachan, provides a perfect foreground to the Cuillin massif. Park safely in a nearby layby (NG469315, 787m). Although small, this loch is worth visiting at different seasons and times of day to enjoy the huge variation in lighting. From a knoll on the other side of the road there is a spectacular view over the Red Hills which opens up on the drive towards Sligachan from Drynoch.

Glen Drynoch (G *Droigheannach*, Thorny Place) is another glacial valley with steep sides which taper off to gentle slopes. Its extension to the west, Loch Harport, was scooped out by the same glacier. There are fine views along this

The Cuillin from Carbost

Marsco from Glen Drynoch

road over the Cuillin, especially from just west of Drynoch.

West Minginish At the west end of Glen Drynoch turn left along the B8009 towards Carbost. This single track road gives access to some of the best scenery on Skye. After 1.5mi (2.5km) a sharp left turn leads to Glen Brittle and the west side of the Cuillin Ridge. Carbost itself is home to Talisker Distillery and the Oyster Shed. Continue along the B8009 to explore Portnalong, Ardtreck Point, and Fiskavaig.

A side road starting from the Carbost war memorial gives access to Talisker Bay, perhaps Skye's finest beach. Glen Eynort is reached by following a signposted fork off this road.

Harta Corry from Marsco

MARSCO (736M)

Sligachan Route Take the footpath signposted to Loch Coruisk on the east side of the bridge. Follow this path along the bottom of Glen Sligachan for 2,800m until Allt an Measarroch is reached on the left. Follow the burn upwards. A line of old metal posts follows on the other side. After about 2,400m, the fence and path turn steeply south up towards the summit ridge.

The summit is 500m northwest. It affords dramatic views over the Cuillin, Glen Sligachan, Beinn Dearg, and Glamaig. To the south, Loch Scavaig and Blaven stand out. A short walk to the west side of the ridge reveals even more of Glen Sligachan. Great care needs to be taken on the steep slopes, especially after rain (9mi, 14km, 736m, 6h).

HARTA CORRY

From Sligachan, follow the footpath signposted Loch Coruisk but keep straight on at Allt na Measarroch. Cross at the watershed between the Lochan Dubha. The Bloody Stone is about 500m to the southwest. Continue westwards into Harta Corry for extremely dramatic views of Lota Corry, Sgurr na Gillean, Am Blasteir, and other peaks. (10mi, 16km, 100m, 4-5h).

Minginish & Cuillin - Minginis

Loch Brittle

Loch Brittle is 9mi (14km) south of Carbost along a single track road. There are spectacular views of the north side of the Cuillin Ridge from various viewpoints along the way.

An extensive sandy beach is exposed at low tide, from which Mussels can be gathered in the proximity of the river mouth.

The Fairy Pools

From the carpark (payment charge, toilets) take the signposted path to Allt Coir' a'Mhadaidh. Cross the stream then follow it for c.1200m to the first waterfall. Further waterfalls and magical pools are revealed as the path winds upwards into Coire na Creiche. Heavy rain may make the route impassable; in a dry spell the flow may reduce to a mere trickle.

The Fairy Pools are most impressive, especially on a sunny evening after rain. Coire na Creiche was the site of the last clan battle in Skye in 1601. It was the culmination of the War of the One Eyed Woman; it ended with the MacDonalds routing the MacLeods.

Coire Lagan & Eas Mór

Eas Mór (G Big Waterfall, NG419214) plunges over a cliff about 900m from Glenbrittle House. A path runs from here to a good viewpoint from where the Huisgill Burn spectacularly plunges 70m. This can be combined with the walk to Coire Lagan.

Coire Lagan is one of the most spectacular of the Cuillin corries. From east of the campsite a good path goes uphill across the moor. A steep gully must be negotiated shortly before reaching the small loch at the centre of this vast natural amphitheatre. The massive vertical cliffs and great splays of rock debris are simply awesome, 6mi, 9km, 500m, 4h.

The Fairy Pools, Glenbrittle

There are dramatic routes into corries at the heart of the Cuillin, Skye's best waterfall and a coastal walk replete with archaeology, dramatic views and wildlife, including Otters. With ever changing light and a sea breeze which limits the midgies, remote Loch Brittle is one of the best places to stay for a few days on Skye.

Loch na h-Airde Viking canal

Coire Lagan

Rubh' an Dùnain

Rubh' an Dùnain (G Point of the Small Fort) faces the southern entrance to Loch Brittle. Apart from having to ford several streams, this is an easy walk; after heavy rain they may be impassable. A good path goes from east of the campsite for most of the way to a ruined settlement.

MacAskills A dyke crosses the headland at Slochd Dubh (G Black Ditch), a natural feature. The ruined house belonged to the MacAskills, the local tacksmen. It was still occupied in 1860; when it was cleared for sheep.

Neolithic Age The best preserved Neolithic chambered cairn in Skye is at the head of the loch. Excavated in the 1930s, the chamber, entrance passage, and courtyard all survive intact.

Dùn An Iron Age promontory fort (NG396159) stands on a small headland, east of the loch; 30m long, it survives to nearly 5m high. A gallery can be seen at one end. The ends of the fort are slowly collapsing into the sea.

Vikings A canal with well-built stone sides flows into Loch na h-Airde from the sea. Traditionally, this was built by the Vikings, who used the loch as a harbour. A timber boat plank found in the loch was dated to c.1100. There are two boat nausts on the north side of the canal as well as stone wharfs on either side of the loch entrance. (8mi, 13km, 3-4h, mostly level walking)

Minginish & Cuillin - Minginis

The Cuillin from Carbost with Talisker Distillery

CARBOST (ON *Karis Bolstaðir*, Kari's Farm) is a small settlement on the south side of Loch Harport. The Old Inn is a popular pub with good bar food and outdoor seating for nice days. Live music sessions are frequent. The Stop Shop is a general store and filling station.

Loch Harport (ON *Hafra Fjordr*, Goat Firth) is a steep-sided glacial valley with extensive salt flats at its head. Many species of waders feed here at low tide, especially during the migration season.

The Oyster Shed is on a steep little lane above the distillery. This unique shop cum takeaway is not to be missed by anyone who loves seafood. Oysters from the owner's farm, lobster, crab, prawns, mussels, scallops, and other seafood are available to takeaway, or to eat outside whilst enjoying views of the Cuillin.

Portnalong (G Harbour for Ships) at the end of the B8009 2.5mi (4km) north of Carbost, has a slip for creel boats. After WWI, the Department of Agriculture created new crofts here for families from Lewis, Harris, and Scalpay. They took their looms with them and a thriving weaving industry developed. *Portna-Skye Tweed* was very popular in the 1930s. The industry was successful in the US and Japan but ended in 1968 when the last weaver retired.

Fiskavaig (ON *Fisk Vagr*, Fish Bay) is beautifully situated facing Loch Bracadale. Extensive black sands are exposed at low tide. A class I Pictish sym-

The Oyster Shed

Portnalong

Carbost, Portnalong, Fiskavaig & Ardtreck

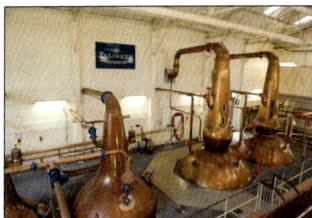
Talisker Distillery

bol stone was found discarded on the tideline here in 1921. The area can be explored on foot via its delightful twisting lanes and coastal footpaths.

Dùn Ardtreck (G *Aird Breac*, Speckled Point NG335358) is a D-shaped broch built on a hillock, whose seaward side is a vertical 20m cliff. The walls are galleried, while the intact entrance retains a lintel, door jambs, and a guard cell. There are two internal doorways leading to probable intramural stairways.

The broch was excavated in the 1960s and dates from c.100BC. Iron tools, bronze objects and Roman Samianware ceramic fragments dated from the 2nd century AD. The site is signposted from the end of a side road in Portnalong.

TALISKER DISTILLERY

Founded in 1830, the distillery now belongs to Diageo, producing c.3m litres annually. The 3 spirit stills (11,024l) and 2 wash stills (14,706l) use worm tube condensers to create the distinctive flavour. Mildly peated malt is from Easter Ross; water comes from nearby springs on Cnoc nan Speireag (G Hawk Hill).

A pier and tramway were built in 1900 to land barley and load casks for shipment. After a fire in 1960 the distillery had to be completely rebuilt. The new stills are exact replicas of the original 1830s designs. Around 40% is matured as single malt, while the rest is used for blending.

Robert Louis Stevenson, in his poem, *The Scotsman's Return From Abroad*, stated, *"The king o' drinks, as I conceive it, Talisker, Isla, or Glenlivet!"*

Tours run all year, except during maintenance. Whisky connoisseurs will want to try the Talisker Tasting Tour. Visitors can appreciate the history and buy a full range of malts.

Fiskavaig

Dùn Ardtreck

Minginish & Cuillin - Minginis

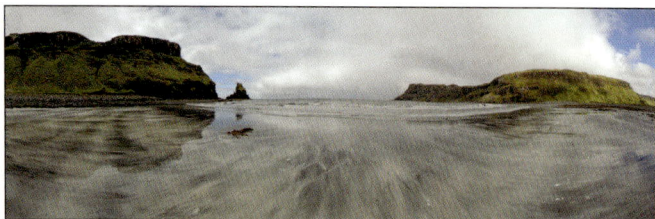

Talisker Bay

TALISKER BAY (ON *Hallr Sker*, Hill-side Skerry, referring to the small stack and steep slope behind it) is perhaps the most romantic of any on Skye. At low tide its streaked black and silver sands, enclosed by steep slopes and cliffs, are very impressive. In the distance the hills of South Uist fill the horizon.

Beach Access Parking (NG326306) near Talisker House on the public road. A sign indicates the route to the bay via a good track. The cliffs here are of particular interest due to their prominent layers of successive lava flows.

Gleann Oraid has spectacular cliffs on the north side formed by an escarpment, Na Huranan on the side of Arnaval (ON *Ern Fjall*, Sea Eagle Hill). The

River Talisker flows through this small but dramatic valley.

Talisker House dates from 1717 and replaced an older 16th century dwelling built by Sir Roderick MacLeod, a great royalist, knighted in 1661. The estate was sold in 1820 when the MacLeods all emigrated to Tasmania. Hugh MacAskill, founder of Talisker Distillery, cleared the area in 1825 for sheep.

Sleadale Broch (NG324292) stands on a rocky knoll above the Sleadale Burn, south of Talisker House. The walls are still up to 2m high in places and about 3m thick with an internal diameter of 12m. The entrance remains intact, with door jambs and a lintel. Intramural galleries can be seen, but the interior is

Gleann Oraid Escarpment

The Cuillin from Loch Eynort

a jumbled mass of stones. Remains of several structures, perhaps shielings, are visible below the broch.

Glen Eynort (ON *Eið Fjordr*, Isthmus Firth) is another glacial valley. It is reached by following a side road off the Carbost to Talisker road.

At Faolainn (ON *Vadill*, flat beach), an ancient graveyard here has two interesting old churches. A chapel dedicated to St Maelrubha is built on the site of a much older one. Nearby, there is a roofless 17th century church. There are several interesting grave monuments here, apart from those removed to the National Museum.

The head of the loch has a large area of salt marsh which is popular with waders

during the migration season. This is also a very good place to seek Otters, especially near the river outfall, either early or late in the day. The meadows and salt marsh are awash with colourful wild flowers in early summer.

PRESHAL BEG & MHÒR

Preshal Beg and Preshal Mhor (ON *Brjòta Fjall*, Broken Hill) are formed from olivine tholeite; a lava. This forms parallel polygonal columns as it cools in a process called columnar jointing. Similar formations exist in Trotternish, the Shiant Islands, Staffa, Mull, and at the Giant's Causeway.

Preashel Beg (NG329279, 347m), the larger of the two features is about 1.5mi (2km) south of Talisker House. Here, broken lava columns lie at the bottom of a high volcanic cliff. The cliffs at nearby Biod Ruadh reach 280m.

Sleadale Broch may be visited en route. It is unusually situated inland with no view of the sea. It overlooks a sheltered valley.

Preshal Beag by William Daniell

Portree Harbour at night

PORTREE

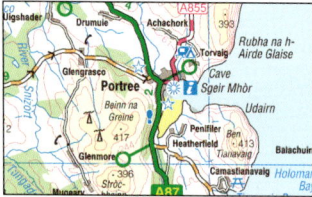

Crown copyright

PORTREE (G *Port Righ*, Port on the Slope, popn. 2,318 in 2011) is situated in a fertile valley facing a sheltered bay. There were few houses here until the start of the 19th century. The Pont map of 1654 shows a building in *"Portray"*, but no settlement or harbour.

King James V embarked on a voyage around Scotland in June 1540 aboard his flagship, *"Salamander"*. Accompanied by twelve other vessels, he landed at Kirkwall and Stornoway before heading to Skye. After visiting Dunvegan and Score Bay, the fleet anchored in Portree harbour. The King and his retinue spent several days here. The local clan chiefs pledged oaths of fealty, the heirs to MacLeod and Clanranald were taken as hostages nevertheless.

It took 414 years before another reigning monarch was to visit Portree, or indeed Skye. Queen Elizabeth, accompanied by the Duke of Edinburgh and Princess Margaret, landed at Kyle from the *"Britannia"* before being driven to Portree, and then Dunvegan Castle for tea with strawberries and cream.

Portree Market was established in c.1580 when a licence was granted by King James VI for a biannual fair. Cattle, horses, sheep and agricultural produce were the main items sold. By 1650 the trade in black cattle had become a major export business. They were shipped in from the Outer Hebrides and then driven to Portree. Trotternish was also a major producer. The other market was at Sligachan, for cattle from the west of Skye.

Early Development
There was a brewery here by 1700, associated with the inn. A mill was also operating around the same time and the first church was

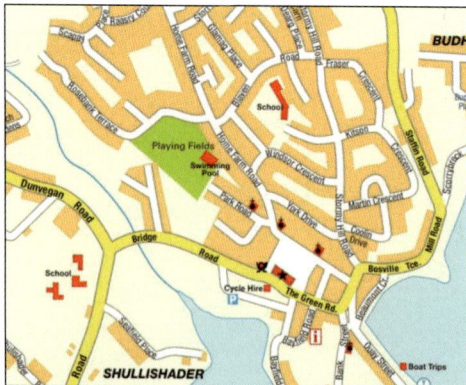

built in the 1730s. Sir James MacDonald proposed extensive plans in 1765 but due to his premature death, only a school was built.

By 1800 the jail, prominent in Daniell's 1815 print, was complete and rows of cottages were springing up. Today the jail serves as Skye's Visitor Information Centre. From here the very helpful staff provide all manner of assistance for tourists. This is a good place to start a visit; maps, guides and many leaflets are available.

The Harbour Front was created at the same time as the road network was built under Thomas Telford. Although there was no pier in 1815, by 1818 Thomas Telford's plans were being put into effect. By 1826, there were regular steamboat services which for the first time opened Portree and Skye up to visitors. This marked the start of tourism for the island as well as making the export of animals much easier.

Portree winter sunrise

Portree by William Daniell, 1815

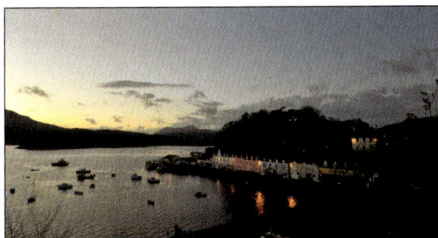

MacNab's Inn stood on the site of the present Royal Hotel. Established in the early 17th century, it was for long the only public house on Skye. It was here that Flora MacDonald bade farewell to Bonnie Prince Charlie on the night of 30th June 1746. She had arranged for a small boat to take him over to Raasay.

PORTREE
ORIGIN OF THE NAME

Early mentions of the town now called "Portree" are in Timotheo Pont's Atlas of 1654 when it was spelt "Portry"; in 1493 it was referred to as "Portray".

WJ Watson, in *History of the Celtic Placenames of Scotland* (1926), *"Portree in Skye is often pronounced in Gaelic "Port-righ", as if "King's Port" and the name is supposed to date from a visit of James V in 1540. The unsophisticated Gaelic pronunciation of Skyemen, however, is "Portrigeadh", and the second part is clearly from righ or ruigh, 'forearm,' common in our place-names as 'slope,' 'ground sloping up to a hill'. "Port Righ" thus means "The Port Below the Slope,"* which perfectly fits its location.

Portree

Portree in the 19th century

The Lump, or Meall, is a small promontory on the south side of the harbour. This was the site of the local gallows for many years. The last execution here took place in June 1742 after a man called Angus Buchanan had been found guilty of the murder of a chapman or peddler. Apparently *"He was hung from the gallows with the greatest decency and without the least disturbance."*`

In the 1820s Dr Alexander MacLeod, or Dr Ban as he was known, planted trees here. He built a folly from which there is a fine view of Portree. Macleod was Chamberlain of Skye, the local factor and a medical doctor. He was highly influential in the development of 19th century Portree.

Skye Games Dr Ban founded the Skye Games in 1825, but they only became a regular fixture on the calendar in 1877. Now called *"The Skye Highland Games"* the event is held in early August each year. *"The Games are one of the highlights of the Skye calendar and are enjoyed by thousands of visitors each year as well as the local population who come from all corners of the island, and beyond, to witness or to participate in this authentic expression of Highland tradition and culture."*

The Town Centre of Portree owes its layout and fine buildings to the MacDonalds. Names such as Wentworth Street and Bosville Terrace came from their marriages to English women. None of the streets in the older part of Portree have Gaelic names, perhaps reflecting the cosmopolitan nature of the people settling here in the 19th century.

Eating and Drinking Portree has a large range of hotels, restaurants, cafes, bars, and chip shops to suit every pocket

Portree evening light

Portree harbour front

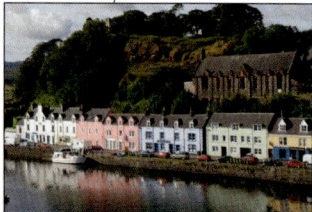

and taste. Particularly recommended are the tiny Scorrybreac Restaurant, Café Arriba, The Granary, Sea Breezes, and The Chippy. During busy periods it is essential to reserve.

Portree and the Storr from the south

Shopping For its size, Portree has a good selection of shops. These include a butcher, fishmonger, fresh fruit and vegetables, a bakery, and specialist outlets. Some are hard to find, on the industrial estate.

There are two bookshops, a visitor information centre, giftshops, and an outdoors shop. High quality local jewellery, tweed garments, craft items, and other goods made on Skye are all available. For supermarkets, the Coop still reigns.

The Aros Experience (ON *A Ros*, River Mouth) is on Viewfield Road, the southern approach to Portree. *"A popular visitor attraction and community cultural centre with exhibitions, cinema, live music, comedy, dance, drama, theatre, galleries and workshops. With a family friendly res-*

taurant, gift shop and children's play areas." There is an admission fee for the exhibition area. Aros has a full programme of events throughout the year in its auditorium, which is Skye's only cinema.

Portree Community Library adjoins Portree High School. It is part of the Fingal Centre which has a swimming pool and sports centre. The Skye and Lochalsh Archive Centre is also located here. It holds regular exhibitions and is the place to start researching family history.

Fishing Industry The catching of Salmon and Sea Trout in the sea was formerly a substantial business on Skye. Portree was well situated for this due to the Varragill River, which was an

Portree Harbour

Fishing boats in Portree Harbour

Portree

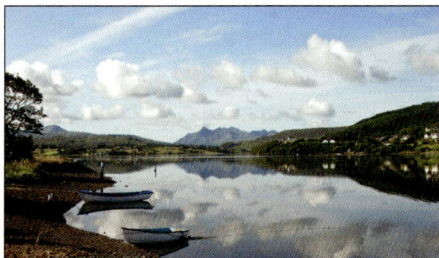
Loch Portree and the Cuillin

tailed Sea Eagles, which nest on cliffs nearby, are the main attraction, Golden Eagles, Common Seals, dolphins, Otters and Porpoises are also often observed. Sea angling, special photography trips, and private charters are also available.

extremely productive Salmon hatchery. The fish were caught in large nets placed at right angles to the shore.

An icehouse still stands on Quay Brae. There were similar fishing stations near river mouths all over Skye. No Salmon are caught commercially now but, at its peak in 1957, nearly 10,000 fish were caught.

Today a number of small inshore vessels catch mostly prawns, crabs, lobsters and scallops. Portree is a Designated Landing Port, but most locally caught whitefish gets landed in Mallaig.

Boat Trips several operators offer boat trips from Portree Harbour. White-

Loch Portree was formerly known as *Loch Chalium-cille*, in reference to the ancient chapel on the estuary of the River Varragill. The tidal mudflats and saltmarsh are very attractive to waders during the bird migration seasons.

Many colourful salt tolerant wild flowers also create colour here in late spring and summer. These include Thrift, Scurvy Grass, Sea Campion, Sea Aster, Sea Rocket, and Buckshorn Plantain. The best access is from the Peinmore road to Inveralivaig on the south side of the bay.

Scorrybreac (ON *Skor Brekka*, Valley Slope) on the slopes of Torvaig (ON *Thor's Vik*, Thor's Bay) was for centuries

Icehouse and Fish n' Chips

Portree B&B

the seat of the Nicholsons of Scorrybreac. Norman, the last chief, emigrated to Tasmania in 1825. The Nicholsons were said to be the oldest clan on Skye. Their old house was demolished c.1827 and the lands cleared for sheep.

Scorrybreac

Ben Chracaig (ON *Kráka Vik*, Crow Bay, 149m) was purchased by Clan MacNicol in 1987. The 52ha are maintained by *Urras Clann MhicNeacail* and local volunteers.

Fairy Cattle, or *Crodh Sìth*, used to come ashore every day from their sea home to enjoy the lush pastures of Scorrybreac. Their fairy owner called them home every evening and they headed back to the shore. One day a man took soil from a nearby churchyard and threw it between the cattle and the sea. This sacred barrier stopped them from hearing their fairy owner's calls. Unable to return to the sea, the cattle had to stay ashore and became part of the herds belonging to humans. Thus did Skye cattle acquire

the fairy blood that made them so outstanding and in high demand in the past.

Portree Post Office

SCORRYBREAC WALK

This circular walk 2mi, 3km, on good footpaths starts near the Cuillin View Hotel with several places to park. Follow the road to a footbridge. A Clan Nicholson memorial commemorates their purchase of this headland in 1987. From here a path heads up to a viewpoint on Ben Chracaig.

The coastal route continues past Murdo's Well, "*built in memory of those of Clan Nicolson who died for their countries in the cause of justice.*"

At a drystone dyke bear left up a steep hill where the path zigzags before reaching level ground. Descend through a small Birch wood before reaching the start. The ruins of Bile Chapel (G *Beal* Cattle Pasture) lie above the shore in lush grassland; the cattle here may be *Crodh Sìth*.

CENTRAL SKYE

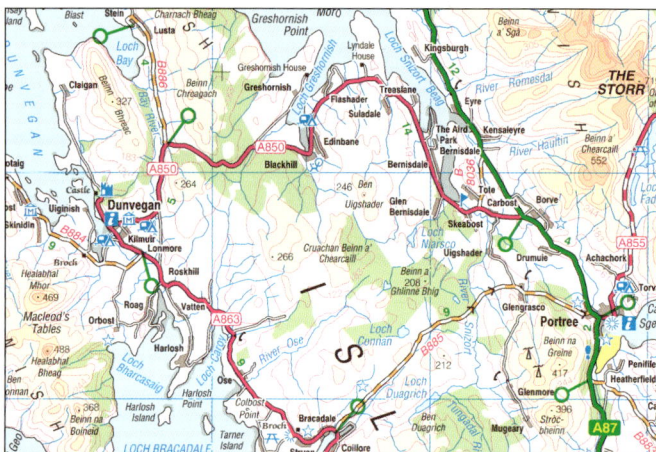

Crown copyright

CENTRAL SKYE This loop starts at Portree and follows the single-track A885 across the moor via Bracadale to Struan. Here, it joins the A863 to Dunvegan, before taking the A850 to Skeabost and Portree. The distance is c.42mi (67km).

The B885 Portree to Struan road crosses the mainly uninhabited central moorland of Skye. Many small volcanic knolls stand prominent in the heather covered landscape. There are several conifer plantations on the north side of the road. To the south, the Cuillin Ridge stands out in early morning or late evening light.

Bracadale (ON *Brekka Dalr*, Slope Valley) is a steep sided glacial valley through which the Amar River (ON *A Hamar*, Crag River) winds beneath dramatic

Cuillin from B885

Bracadale

Loch Bracadale

cliffs. Bracadale is also the name for the surrounding parish. The Vikings referred to Loch Bracadale as *Vatnafiordr*, or Water Firth.

According to the *Orkneyinga Saga*, there was a great battle here in 1039. Earl Thorfinn and Earl Rognvald were on an expedition that summer. *"They plundered in the Sudreyar and in Ireland and in Scotland's Fiord; and Thorfinn conquered the land wherever he went. The battle began early in the morning and the kinsmen gain victory."*

MacLeods of Gesto

For centuries the lands of Gesto were owned by the MacLeods, not by Dunvegan. This ended in 1674, when MacLeod of Gesto took out a tack (lease) from MacLeod of MacLeod. "Gesto" was drinking and gambling with his brother in law, MacAskell of Ebost, and the heir to Dunvegan.

After an excess of alcohol, a serious argument arose during which Gesto challenged MacAskell to a duel. The latter died in the ensuing sword fight. Gesto was found guilty of murder and as a result his lands were declared forfeit. The family bad feeling festered for many years until, in 1825, MacLeod refused to renew the tack.

Struan (G Small Stream) is a small settlement on the west side of Bracadale. This whole area is strewn with prehistoric remains. Neolithic chambered cairns, at least six brochs, and an Iron Age souterrain all lie within a short distance, perhaps emphasising the importance of Loch Harport in former times.

Loch Bracadale

Struan

Central Skye

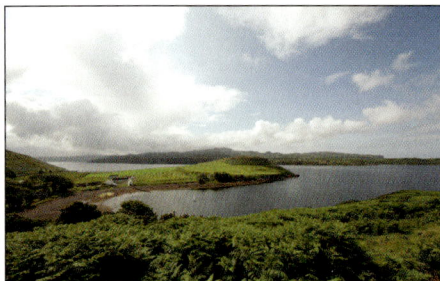
Gesto

Gesto (ON *Gestr Haugr*, Guest Mound) was occupied by a cadet branch of the MacLeods for about 500 years. Gesto House stands abandoned and roofless, having been vacated by the MacLeods after the tack, or lease, was made over to sheep farmers from the Borders. The impressive model steading was built in the 19th century.

Dùn Taimh overlooks this pretty little bay and peninsula from the top of nearby Beinn Dubh. This ancient fort encloses a slightly incongruous cairn celebrating Queen Victoria's 50th Jubilee in 1887.

Sumardale (ON *Sunn Moerr Dalr*, South March) marks the west end of an ancient border between Bracadale and Minginish. Although the name is Norse, the parish boundary may be much older.

Dùn Beag (G Small Fort) is an Iron Age broch, about 500m west of Struan at the turning for Ullinish. There is a signposted carpark from which a path goes uphill for about 200m to the prominently sited broch. The monument is in the care of Historic Environment Scotland.

This broch is one of the best-preserved on Skye and also the most accessible. It clearly exhibits most of the characteristics of these buildings, which are unique to the north of Scotland and the islands.

Dùn Mór (G Big Fort) is about 500m further inland on the edge of a low escarpment. The summit is surrounded by low cliffs, except on the northeast side.

Loch Bracadale and the Cuillin Ridge

Dùn Mór and the Cuillin

Although interpreted by some as an Iron Age fort, this monument is probably a much older Neolithic chambered cairn. The remains of at least two chambers can be seen. The well-built terminal wall faces appear to have forecourts, similar to Campston Long Cairn in Caithness.

The fertile valley to the south of this escarpment is criss-crossed with ancient field walls. There are also a number of probable ruins of houses. From here a panoramic view extends from the Cuillin Ridge and over Loch Bracadale, to MacLeod's Tables in the west.

Ullinish (ON *Ullis Nes*, Ulli's Point) is an attractive low headland with a loop road opposite Dùn Beag. Ullinish Lodge is an 18th century farmhouse and now a highly rated small hotel. Dinner here is simply excellent, as one reviewer put it, "*This restaurant (with rooms) is the ultimate in gourmet dining. The evening meals are the best I have ever tasted during a three nights stay.*"

Oronsay (ON *Orifsey*, Ebb-tide Island) lies just south of Ullinish Point. It can

---

DÙN BEAG

Dùn Beag is one of c.100 brochs, galleried duns and similar Iron Age buildings in Skye. It is perched on a volcanic hillock with steep cliffs on three sides. The broch survives to over 2m, has an external diameter of 18m and walls 4m thick at the foundations.

The entrance has no lintel, but retains its door jambs; there are no guard cells. An intramural stairway leads to a second level. To the right there is a small cell; opposite the doorway there is an intramural passage.

The interior was cleared out before 1920. Stone tools, pottery and metal objects from various periods were found. The broch may date from c.400BC but continued to be inhabited until the late 18th century; on the basis of coins with various dates.

---

be reached via a signposted path which starts opposite Ullinish Lodge. A causeway ebbs dry by about half tide, allowing access. For such a small island, Oronsay has much to offer, including sandy

Dùn Beag overlooks Loch Bracadale

CENTRAL SKYE

Harlosh

St John's Chapel is a small Episcopalian chapel which was consecrated in 1838 but abandoned by 1855. The graveyard is still in use and has several interesting headstones. Most poignant is that of Flora MacDonald Margaret Swire, killed when PanAm flight 103 was blown up over Lockerbie in December 1988.

beaches, fine views, rock stacks, a natural arch, and a cave. There is even an old fish trap at the end of the causeway.

Ose (ON *Óss*, River Mouth) is a small settlement at the estuary of the River Ose, a large burn which flows into the east side of Loch Caroy. At low tide shingly mudflats are exposed which are popular with waders during the migration seasons.

Caroy (G *Cadha Ruadh*, Red Rock) takes its name from the colour of its volcanic rocks. A ruined broch overlooks the bay from a knoll on its east side.

She was the granddaughter of Otta Swire, the author of "*Skye, the Island and its Legends.*" Flora Swire was directly descended from the Flora MacDonald who became famous in 1746 due to her involvement in the escape of Bonnie Prince Charlie after Culloden.

Chambered Cairns Two prominent mounds just west of Caroy are Neolithic chambered cairns. Both are built from large numbers of stones, large and small. The cairns appear to be intact and have never been excavated.

Ullinish

Caroy Chambered Cairn

MacLeod's Maidens

Harlosh (ON *Hafra Bolstaðir*, Billy Goat Farm) is a low peninsula with a loop road. There are fine views over Loch Vatten to MacLeod's Maidens from Camas Bàn. This may be the *Vatnafiordr* mentioned in the *Orkneyinga Saga* battle of 1039 where Orkney Viking Earls fought a mighty battle.

Ancient sites include a broch, Dùn Feorlig, facing Loch Caroy, a promontory fort, Dùn Néill, and an ancient chapel site, both near Harlosh Point. This small headland is well worth exploring.

Horneval (ON *Orn Fjall*, Sea-eagle Hill) is a farm on the side road which

MacLeod's Maidens

Idrigill Point (ON *Ytri Gill*, Outer Ravine) forms the southeasterly tip of Duirinish. MacLeod's Maidens is a group of three rock stacks, the largest of which is 70m tall. They are said to represent the wife and daughters of a MacLeod, who were lost at sea.

Walk Park at Orbost Farm then follow a track around Loch Bharcasaig and head left through woodland. Idrigill has many ruined houses and extensive lazy beds. Continue through Glac Ghealaridh to Rubha na Maighdeanan and the Maidens. Total distance c.11mi, 18km; allow 6h.

cuts across the moor from the A863 to the A850 just south of Dunvegan. There are fine views of MacLeod's Maidens and Duirinish from here. Ben Horneval (264m) itself overlooks the A850 from the east and offers even better views.

MacLeod's Tables from Horneval

CENTRAL SKYE

Loch Bracadale from Ullinish

Orbost (*Orris Bolstaðir*, Orri's Farm) was the home of the author and folklorist Otta Swire, who lived in the house from 1946 to 1973. Born here in 1898, she spent her life collecting ancient tales.

Loch Bharkasaig (ON *Virki Vagr*, Rampart Bay) is named after a long disappeared Norse or Iron Age fortification which was once here, possibly on Meall Greepa (G Precipice Hill). There are excellent views from this headland.

Greshornish (ON *Grice Nes*, Pig's Point) is a remote and ruggedly beautiful peninsula. A walk around the headland followed by lunch at the Greshornish House Hotel is a pleasant way to spend a day in this part of Skye. There are clear paths for most of the way, 4mi, 6km, 4h.

Edinbane (G *An t-aodann Ban*, Fair Face, perhaps from Bog Cotton), the A850 bypasses it, making it a tranquil village. The Edinbane Inn is reckoned to be one of the best pubs on Skye. There is a pottery, a shop, and a filling station.

Dùn Suladale (NG375527) is an Iron Age broch situated on a rock outcrop 100m above Loch Snizort. The walls still reach 2.4m in height and 3.7m wide. The entrance passage faces northwest and retains four lintels and a guard cell. An intramural stairway leads to the now collapsed second level.

Around the broch, the ruins of buildings and field walls are prominent. It is about 800m southwest of the A850. Follow the side road to Suladale and then strike

Greshornish

Pictish Stone at Tote

across the moor. There are glorious views to the Outer Hebrides and south to the Cuillin.

Skeabost (ON *Skeið Bolstaðir*, Horse Racing Farm) is at the head of Loch Snizort. St Columba's Isle is surrounded by two branches of the River Snizort. Here, the saint

Skeabost River

is said to have proselytised from a rock. This was probably an ancient religious site long before the arrival of Columba.

Under Norse rule there was a bishop's see at Skeabost from the 11th century, under the Archbishop of Nidaros, now Trondheim. By the 12th century, the church here was known as the Cathedral of the Bishops of the Isles. In 1349 the bishop no longer had to report personally to Nidaros.

The Cathedral was still standing in 1501, but was demolished during the reformation. Today, only the footings remain of what must have been a sub-stantial church. A small roofless 11th century chapel dedicated to St Columba stands to the west. This may have been contemporary with the Cathedral, or even earlier.

Many generations of Nicholson Chieftains are said to be buried here. There are several interesting medieval carved grave slabs, as well as ancient grave markers. The whole island is a place apart and it has a very peaceful feeling.

Pictish Stone The Pictish Symbol Stone at nearby Tote suggests that the Snizort area may have been an important religious centre for a long time.

Skeabost Cathedral site

Neist Point sunset, Durinish

Dunvegan - Dùn Bheagain

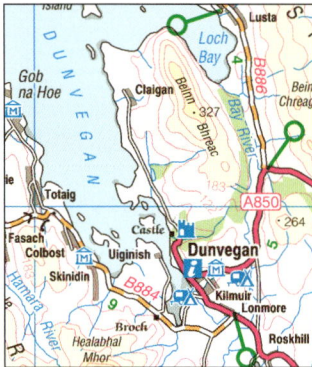

Crown copyright

DUNVEGAN CASTLE is deservedly the most popular visitor attraction on Skye. MacLeod of MacLeod sums it up well, *"Any visit to the enchanted Isle of Skye must be deemed incomplete without savouring the wealth of history offered by Dunvegan Castle"*

Dunvegan (G *Dùn*, ON *Bekan*, Bekan's Fort or perhaps ON *Avaig*, ON ship, G *bheag*, small Fort of the small ships, as at Dunnyveg in Islay). Whatever the truth, the name *"Dunvegan"* is redolent of the Norse-Gael heritage of the MacLeods.

The oldest visible parts of the castle date from the 13th century. They include original sections of the curtain wall and the base of the Fairy Tower. The well is much older; there was almost certainly an earlier Norse keep here and a broch during the Iron Age.

The Castle Rock is a flat-topped basalt stack, about 54m by 34m and 12m high. A deep ravine separates it from the rest of the coast, through which the sea once flowed at high tide. Until 1748, the only entrance was by the Sea Gate. Ancient rock cut steps lead to the shore on the northwest side.

Although the castle today appears to look like one building from a distance, in fact this is the result of Victorian "romantic restoration". There are six buildings, built in at least ten phases, with much modification and repairs.

The Fairy Flag, *"the most treasured possession of the Clan"* is on display in the Drawing Room. *"The fabric, thought once to have been dyed yellow, is silk from the Middle East (Syria or Rhodes); experts have dated it between the 4th and*

Dunvegan Castle from Uiginish

7th centuries AD, in other words, at least 400 years before the First Crusade. So was it the robe of an early Christian saint? Or the war banner of Harold Hardrada, King of Norway, killed in 1066, or did it emerge mysteriously from some grassy knoll in Skye?"

Dunvegan Castle from seaward side

Other interesting artefacts include the Dunvegan Cup, Rory Mór's Horn, MacCrimmon Bagpipes and items left by Flora MacDonald. Self-guided tours start in the Front Hall and are best taken at a leisurely pace as there is much of interest to see. The excellent guide book is strongly recommended.

The Gardens were first developed in the early 19th century, but mostly date from the 1970s. They are at their best in early summer. From February onwards, Snowdrops, Primroses, Daffodils, and Bluebells provide early colour. There are many interesting plants from New Zealand, Japan, Korea, Chile, and the United States. To enjoy the gardens to the full, it is necessary to spend at least a couple of hours exploring their many aspects.

Opening Dates The Castle and Gardens are open daily from April to mid-October. There are open days for viewing Snowdrops in February.

Dunvegan Castle entrance

Fairy Flag and relics

Dunvegan Castle

Dunvegan - Dùn Bheagain

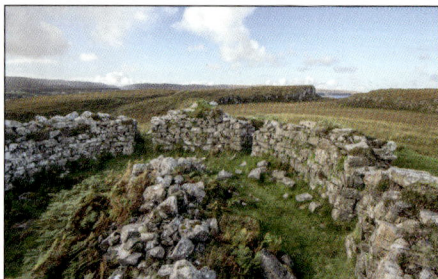
Dùn Fiadhairt

Dùn Fiadhairt (G *Fiadhairt*, Good Land, NG231504) is one of at least eight Iron Age brochs and forts in the Dunvegan area. It is built on a rocky knoll in the middle of a small peninsula. This is joined to the rest of Skye by a narrow neck. There are excellent views in all directions as well as significant remains of ancient drystone dykes, including an imposing entrance gateway.

This galleried broch is 16.8m in diameter with walls c.3.4m thick which still stand over 2m high. The interior is a perfect circle, 9.5m in diameter. The main entrance faces southwest. It has no lintels but retains door checks, holes for the bar, and has two guard cells. There is a long intramural (c.21m) gallery and the remains of a stairway.

Part of a scarcement survives to the left of the doorway, indicating that the first floor was c.2m above the ground. There is a small second doorway opposite the entrance. Whether this is original is unclear.

The most interesting artefact found was a Roman votive (religious) object, a small clay model of a bale of wool. Glass and amber beads, Iron Age pottery, stone tools, and "iron refuse" were found, but no bronze or coins. It was excavated in 1892 in the manner of the times.

Dùn Fiadhairt can be reached from the south end of Loch Suardal on the road from Dunvegan to Claigan. Park near the loch; from here a locked gate gives access to a good track which passes through rich pasture to the isthmus.

Dùn Fiadhairt

Claigan souterrain

Seals The largest Common Seal colony on Skye inhabits the southern shores of Fiadhairt and also nearby Gairbh Island. They can be approached closely by keeping quiet and moving discretely. Boat tours from Dunvegan Castle also visit this area.

Coral Beach and Lampay

The Coral Beaches are a short walk north of Claigan (G *Cladhach*, Cultivated Field). This curved expanse of maerl and seashells is sheltered by Lampay to the west and Cnoc Mór Ghrobain to the east. They are deservedly very popular with visitors. Many regard this beach as the best on Skye. There is an excellent panoramic view from the hill behind.

The "coral" is in fact produced by seaweeds called *Lithothamnion glaciale* and *Phymatolithon calcareum*; coralline algae which form large beds offshore. In life they are a dark pink colour. Tidal currents and wave action break up the skel-

Coral Beach

etons of dead maerl which are washed ashore and bleached by the sun.

Claigan Souterrain is an Iron Age underground passage, probably the cellar of a roundhouse. From the Coral Beach carpark head up the hill on a farm road to a sharp right hand bend. The entrance is behind a bank on the left side of the road (NG238539). Waterproof trousers and a torch are essential. The passage is 10m long and slopes gently upwards.

Coral Beaches

From Dunvegan Castle, follow a minor road north for 3.5mi (5km) to a carpark. The Coral beaches are signposted. Follow the coast to Camas Bàn, cross a burn and go through a gap in a stone dyke. The Coral Beaches are revealed from a hillock. Lampay is joined to Skye by a tombola which is exposed at low tide, 2.5mi, 4km, 1h walk but allow 3h.

DUNVEGAN - DÙN BHEAGAIN

Loch Dunvegan and the Cuillin Ridge from Uiginish

DUNVEGAN is a small township extending along the southeast head of Loch Dunvegan at the junction of the roads to Portree and Sligachan. Most of the buildings are 19th century, as are the croft strips between Lonmore and Kilmuir.

Piers Dunvegan has probably always been a harbour. The first pier was built by Thomas Telford in 1815, at the same time as the roads. The present one was constructed in 1865. Steamers called here regularly for many years, leading to the development of hotels in the 1860s. Today, creel boats, Salmon farm workboats, and yachts are the main traffic, along with small cruise ships.

St Mary's Church (Kilmuir) dates from 1694. It was abandoned in 1832 and ruinous by the 1860s. There are many 18th century funerary monuments. The MacCrimmons, who were pipers to the MacLeods for 13 generations, are buried here.

Duirinish Stone This 5m monolith was erected in June 2000 to celebrate the millennium. It stands at the south end of the Druim na Creige ridge, overlooking Dunvegan. There are fine views to MacLeod's Tables and of the distant Cuillin Ridge to the south.

Duirinish Parish Church was built in 1832 in the style of the time, dubbed by some as *"Carpenter's Gothick"*. The interior fittings are all original, with wooden pews, a gallery, and an elaborate pulpit. There is a fine signposted walk which takes in the two churches and the standing stone.

MacLeod's Tables from Dunvegan

St Mary's Church

Loch Head The estuary of Allt an Loin Mhor and the River Osdale has a large area of saltmarsh and mudflats. Herons and Otters are often seen here. In late spring and summer the shoreline is coloured by Scurvy Grass, Thrift, Spring Squill, Maritime Plantain, and Sea Aster.

Sunset down Loch Dunvegan

Waders and waterfowl are also attracted here during migration periods.

Dùn Osdale overlooks Dunvegan from the southwest. This ruined Iron Age broch is sited just beside the road at the turn off for Uiginish, and is worth the short climb for the panoramic view alone. It is one of at least eight in this immediate area, suggesting the strategic importance of Loch Dunvegan over 2,000 years ago.

Uiginish Viewpoint A side road signposted to Uiginish ends at the eponymous 18th century tacksman's house and farm. Follow a track to the top of Cnocan Leathan, a hillock about 500m to the north. There are wonderful views of Dunvegan Castle and down the loch to the Cuillin Ridge. The mudflats and saltmarshes can be observed and accessed from this side road.

Facilities Dunvegan offers a wide range of accommodation, restaurants, cafes, and shops. It is a good base from which to explore the spectacular north and west of Skye. Neist Point, Waternish, and Bracadale are only a short distance away. This area is famous for its summer sunsets. In winter, dark skies allow the stars and Milky Way to be seen and perhaps the aurora.

Allt an Loin Mhór estuary

Dunvegan saltmarshes

Duirinish · Diùirinis

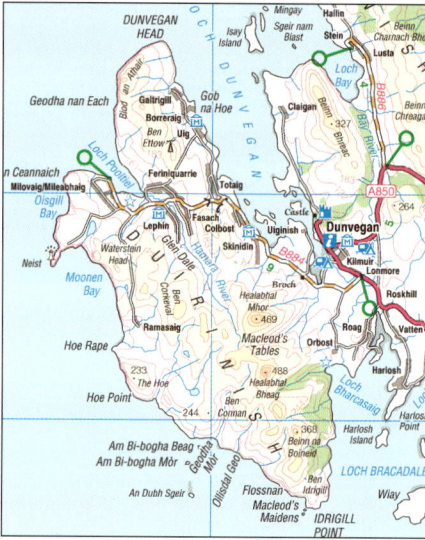

Crown copyright

MacLeod's Tables Healabhal Mhor (468m) and Healabhal Beag (488m, ON *Hjalli Fjall*, Terraced Hill) dominate the skyline for miles around. These flat topped hills were formed by serial lava flows and shaped by ice. Haeval Mhór features in the famous MacLeod wager.

Colbost (ON *Kolls Bolstaðir*, Koll's Homestead) is a small crofting township on the west shore of Loch Dunvegan. It is overlooked by Dùn Colbost, an Iron Age Broch.

Colbost Croft Museum is a blackhouse, once so common on Skye. It has thick drystone walls and a thatched roof, but no chimney. A peat fire burns in a central hearth, smoke escapes through the roof. The furnishings are typical of the 19th century. They include a box bed, dresser, tables and chairs. There are various old

Duirinish (ON *Dyr Nes*, Deer Ness) is the most northwesterly of Skye's peninsulas. In Gaelic, the local folk are nicknamed *Na Moganaich*; Duirinish is known as *Dùthaich nam Mogan*. This may refer to the prowess of the local young men in battle. *Mogan* can mean young hero, or raw, unmatured whisky.

MacLeod's Tables from Dunvegan

Colbost Croft Museum

tools, implements, and newspaper articles about the clearances and crofters.

The Three Chimneys is as different as it is possible to be from the Museum. Eddie and Shirley Spear developed the business for over 30 years. With a global reputation, it has won many awards. It is now under new ownership.

Borreraig (ON *Borgar Vik*, Broch Bay) is the former seat of the legendary Mac-Crimmons. Their Piping College was established here in c.1500, and continued for nearly 300 years. Overgrown ruins can still be seen today below the road near a memorial cairn (NG189536).

Like so many things on Skye, the fairies had a lot to do with the wonderful music

Colbost

MacLeod's Wager

Clan Chieftain Alasdair Crotach MacLeod was at Court in Edinburgh in c.1500, and was suitably impressed by the grandeur. At a banquet where much drink was consumed, he was taunted, *"You never saw such a large table as this in the Islands"*, *"Did you ever see such candlesticks in Skye?"*, *"How do you entertain your guests in Skye?"*, or *"Have you such a hall as this?"* MacLeod responded, *"If you do me the honour to visit me at Dunvegan I will show you a larger table and far finer candlesticks than any here, and a better banqueting hall, too.*

"A wager, a wager, and we accept, we will visit you at Dunvegan one year from today." *"You will all be welcome"* was MacLeod's dignified response.

His guests duly arrived and were hospitably received. *"Let us see your table, your candlesticks, your banqueting hall that are finer than the King's"*, they urged. *"Tonight we will dine"*, replied MacLeod. He led the way to the flat top of Healaval Beg. On *"MacLeod's Table"*, a banquet was laid out. Behind each guest were stalwart young Mac-Leods with flaming torches.

"This is my table. Can the King in his city show a larger one? These are my candlesticks; brave and faithful followers are worth more than gold. As for my banqueting hall, I dine beneath the canopy of Heaven. Can King James claim a finer ceiling, or equal the stars of God?"

Duirinish · Diùirinis

Biod an Athair (314m) is the highest sea cliff on Skye

that the MacCrimmons played and composed. For centuries they were hereditary pipers to MacLeod of Dunvegan. The farm of Borreraig was held rent free in return. In 1770 Norman MacLeod took back half the land. By 1838, 18 families were paying £100 in total in rent. There was no piping school, and the farm had been split into small crofts.

Galtrigill (ON *Galtr Gill*, Pig's Valley) is about 1mi (1.5km) north of Borreraig, at the road end. There was a substantial settlement here around the Galtrigill Burn before the area was cleared in the 19th century. There are many ruined houses, all surrounded by a curved head dyke, made of turf on a central core of stones. Uphill, there are extensive lazy beds and pastures. Doubtless this settlement was inhabited for millennia.

Biod an Athair (G The Father, or Highest Peak, 314m) is the highest sea cliff on Skye. Its summit is indicated by a trig point about 2,000m from the settlement. There are fine panoramic views from here, but care should be taken near the precipitous cliffs.

Dunvegan Head, in comparison, is quite low. To reach it follow the cliffs

Dunvegan Head from Pooltiel

northeastwards and return to Galtrigill along the coast. There is an interesting natural arch, Am Famhair or The Giant, about halfway back (NG182558). The distance is c.6mi, 9km; allow 4h to explore the ruins and enjoy the views.

Glendale (G *Gleann*, ON *Dalr*, Valley) today is a quietly thriving community owned 7,525ha estate, which covers much of northern Duirinish. During 1882 and 1883 it was the site of a famous and pivotal standoff between the crofters and the landowner, backed by the government.

These actions, publicised by the national press, led directly to the Napier Royal Commission and the Crofters (Holdings) Act, 1886. A cairn and plaque commemorate these events and the activists involved, especially John Mac-Pherson.

Glendale Watermill stands above the estuary of the Hamara River (NG168498). It was renovated in 1970, but was ruinous by 2008. It now has a steel roof but is no longer functional. An overshot millwheel with a wooden lade,

Glendale

as well as millstones, can be seen. Nearby, a small kiln is built into the hillside.

Hamara (ON *Hamar À*, Cliff River) flows through this lush green valley. There are many interesting place names here, including Feriniquaire (G MacQuarrie's Land) and Hameraverin (ON *Hamar Vin*, Crag Pasture) which reflect the mixed Norse-Gaelic heritage.

Loch Pooltiel is said to be named after Diel, a Viking who was drowned here. The small headland of Meanish (ON *Mjo Nes*, Narrow Point) shelters a small harbour and the beach of Milovaig (ON *Mel Vagr*, Sandy Bay), otherwise known as *Traigh Bhàn* (G White Beach). From here there are dramatic views across the bay to the high cliffs of Dunvegan Head, which reach 313m.

Hamara River, Glendale

Loch Pooltiel

DUIRINISH · DIÙIRINIS

Neist Point from the north

Neist Point (ON *Neðsta*, Nethermost Point) is the most westerly headland on Skye. The lighthouse was first lit in 1909 and automated in 1990. The light is 43m above mean sea level on a 19m tower, and flashes every 5 seconds, with a range of 16nm. David A Stevenson was the consulting engineer. The cableway was used for small deliveries; a jetty in a small geo near Camas Bàn is still in use for landing stores.

Waterstein Head (296m) overlooks Moonen Bay (G *Mogan*, Young Hero's Bay) from the east. There are dramatic red high cliffs for over 4mi (6km) to the Hoe (231m). Ramasaig (ON *Hrafn Vik*, Raven Bay) and Lorgill Bay are the only places with access to the sea. There are many remains of settlements in this remote area, which was cleared in 1830.

Loch Mór, is a dramatic foreground to the cliffs. There is a good viewpoint from the hill, with plenty of room to park. The loch is said to be the home of an *Each Uisge*, or Kelpie, which charms young ladies. They are given away by the sand and seaweed in their hair.

From Loch Mór, Allt na h-Uamha (G Burn of the Cave) flows through a steep

Waterstein Head and Moonen Bay

gully into Camas na Sidhean (G Bay of the Fairies), confirming the presence of the supernatural in this enchanting area.

Time to Visit Neist Point is very popular with photographers for sunset and "golden hour" shots. The path around the cliffs from the carpark gives fine panoramic views over the Minch. The best time to go is during or just after a major Atlantic storm. Huge waves crash into the cliffs and over the lighthouse. The path is dangerous in high winds.

Wildlife Neist Point is one of the best sea watching places on Skye. Migrating birds, feeding Gannets, Guillemots, and Razorbills are often present. Basking Sharks may be observed. Minke Whales, Bottlenose and Risso's Dolphin, as well as Orcas are seen close inshore; due to the water depth of 60m or more.

Golden and White-tailed Sea Eagles breed here, as do Ravens. They are most prominent early in the year performing their mating displays. They nest early and are very active whilst hunting to feed their young. All three species are endemic and may be seen year round.

Neist Point lighthouse

Loch Mór

Neist Point

Parking may be difficult at busy times. Do not obstruct other vehicles or access as there is plenty of space.

Lighthouse A steep concrete path goes to the lighthouse. This may be slippery when wet; take care on the precipitous section above Camas na h-Annait. The handrail is corroded and unsafe. The headland is interesting, especially the "secret" sandy beach of Camas Bàn; 2mi, 3km, 2h.

West Cliffs From the carpark take a path to the right, follow the cliff to an old coastguard lookout hut. This was used to monitor shipping movements. The views to the lighthouse are much photographed; you may be alone.

Waterstein Head offers stunning views over Moonen Bay and Neist Point. Few people visit this remote headland, which is about 1,500m from the side road to Ramasaig. There is a fine circular walk along the cliffs from here to Ramasaig; return by the road; marshy in places, several fences to cross; 5mi, 8km, 2-3h.

Sunset over the Minch and Outer Hebrides from Stein, Waternish

Waternish · Bhatairnis

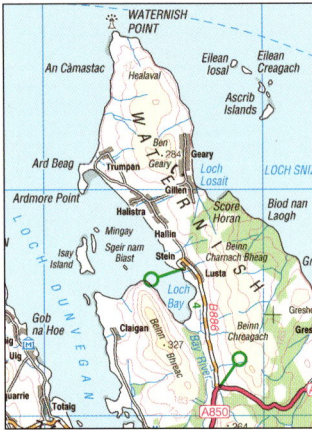

Crown copyright

Waternish (ON *Vatn Nes*, Waterness) is a narrow peninsula between Loch Dunvegan and Loch Snizort. It is reached from the A850, from the Fairy Bridge near Dunvegan.

The Fairy Bridge of today was probably built as part of the new road from Kyle Akin to Stein soon after 1800. The *Sìth*, or fairies, play an important part in the legends and early history of Skye, and none more than the famous Fairy Flag itself. In former times marriages between humans and fairies were quite common.

After an early MacLeod chief's fairy wife gave birth to a son, she had to return to her own folk. The stricken father could only go as far as the Fairy Bridge with her. Before she left she handed MacLeod a little wooden box which contained a magic banner, *"the waving of which would bring forth a host of armed men to help its owner"*. The caveat was that it could only be used three times. The banner is still on display at Dunvegan Castle.

There are many variations on this tale, as well as mysterious happenings in this area. The best time to investigate is on a misty, moonless evening on one's own, preferably after having read Otta Swire.

Annait (NG272527) is an interesting ancient site about 1,300m from the mouth of the Bay River, 1mi (1.5km) north of the Fairy Bridge. It is on a tongue of land with the river to the east, a low cliff to the west and a ravine to the north. The site is c.140m by c.50m and has the remains of massive stone walls, especially on the south side. This wall is over 40m long and c.1.5m high with a

The Fairy Bridge

Stein old pier

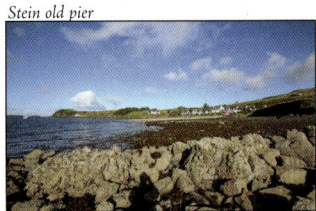

Sunset over Loch Bay from Stein

fine gateway. The wall may have had an intramural gallery.

Several ruined buildings lie within the walls. These could be beehive dwellings, suggesting that there may have been a monastery here. The site is clearly much more ancient, perhaps Iron Age. The term *"Annait"* seems generally to refer to ancient religious sites which were later taken over by early Christian monks.

Stein In 1787 Lochbay was chosen by the British Fisheries Society as the site of one of its planned fishing ports. Land was purchased from the MacLeod at Stein and Lusta. Thomas Telford designed an elegant village, only part of which was completed. The row of whitewashed houses on MacLeod Terrace partly dates from this time. The Stein Inn is said to be the oldest on Skye. The nearby Lochbay Restaurant is well reviewed but book first to avoid disappointment.

Old Pier The original pier was designed by Telford and was one of the first to be built using "Roman cement". This had been invented by James Parker in the 1780s, and has the very useful property of setting within 15 minutes after mixing it with water and sand. All that remains today is a jumble of large cut masonry on the shore south of the present slipway.

Fossils The beach south of the jetty has many limestone rocks which are full of fossils. These comprise mostly bivalve molluscs and are part of the Duntulm Formation. This formed c.150 million years ago in shallow lagoons. Species include Oysters, *Unio* and *Neomiodon*. Small pebbles containing fossils are easily found here.

Skyeskyns, at 17 Lochbay just above Stein, is a tannery specialising in sheepskin. Visitors can watch the whole process of traditional leather making. Sheepskins, leather rugs, clothing, and footwear are on sale in the shop.

Waternish - *Bhatairnis*

Trumpan Church

Trumpan Church, or Kilconan, is situated on a one sided hillock said to resemble a *timpan*; an old fashioned harp. The east gable and north wall still stand intact, but the other walls are down to their foundations. The arched doorway and narrow windows are characteristic of 12th century Norse churches. It may be the only such Norse building in Skye.

Clach Deuchainn (G The Trial Stone) stands in the graveyard. It is about 1.5m high and has a hole in it which was used to assess a person's guilt or innocence. Blindfolded, they had to unhesitatingly insert their finger in the hole. A smaller stone within the church, which may be the font, has a cup shaped hole from which those afflicted with various disorders could drink when seeking a cure. Today people deposit coins.

Ardmore (G *Ard Mór*, Big Headland) is joined to the rest of Skye by a narrow isthmus. There is a shingle bar, or oyce, and a tidal lagoon on the south side. This is one of the best places on Skye to observe the sunset over the Minch and the Outer Hebrides. It is also one of the few good anchorages in Waternish apart from Loch Bay. The lagoon is popular with wildfowl and waders in the migration seasons.

Dùn Hallin (NG257593) is one of the best preserved brochs on Skye. It is on a small plateau on the northwest side of Beinn na Mòintich (176m), about 500m from the side road to Geary. There are panoramic views from here. Two brochs on Loch Dunvegan, and at least two on Trotternish, are visible. From the top of Ben Geary (284m) the other two Water-

Trumpan Church graveyard

Carved graveslab

Sunset over Ardmore

nish brochs can be seen as well as ten or more others.

It still stands to a height of 3.4m, with an internal diameter of c.11m and a thickness of c.3.3m. There is an intramural gallery on the southwest side, as well as the remains of a stairway. The entrance is full of debris but two guard cells remain in reasonable condition. There is also a substantial outer wall about 50m in diameter. Ruined huts and field walls are all around.

Geary (ON Garðr, Farm) Knockbreck and Gillen together make up a long crofting township, with narrow fields running down towards the shore from

THE BATTLE OF THE SPOILING OF THE DYKE

In 1577 a group of MacLeods visiting Eigg committed a terrible atrocity by lighting a smoky fire at the entrance to a cave where all 395 MacDonalds on the island were hiding.

In revenge, one foggy Sunday in May 1578, eight *birlinns* from Uist crept into Ardmore Bay. The people were in Trumpan Church, whose thatched roof was set ablaze. One woman escaped to raise the alarm.

The intruders rounded up as many cattle as they could. This allowed the MacLeods from Dunvegan to sail round and attack the MacDonalds with the aid of the Fairy Flag. A few escaped on a small boat. The dead were buried by toppling a turf dyke on the shoreline over the bodies. This may be legend, but for the roofless church and the cave on Eigg.

the road. From here there are fine views over the Ascrib Islands to Trotternish. This tranquil backwater is a pleasant place to stay for a few days.

Dùn Hallin

Geary and Loch Losalt

WATERNISH · *BHATAIRNIS*

Dùn Borrafiach

About a third of the way along the track to Unish there is a prominent cairn. This commemorates Roderick MacLeod, who fell at the 2nd Battle of Waternish with the MacDonalds of Trotternish, in 1530.

Waternish Point The walk from Trumpan Church to Waternish Point is delightful, with much to see along the way. There are two ruined brochs, settlement remains, a large 17th century farmhouse and fine views over the Minch. The area is quite remote, there are no crowds.

Wildlife With deep water (100m) close inshore, Waternish Point is one of the best places on Skye to look for whales and dolphins. Here, Gannets often dive for fish. Both Golden and White-tailed Sea Eagles are frequently seen quartering the coast for prey, often very close up.

Dùn Borrafiach (G Raven's Broch, NG236637, 130m) is spectacularly sited on a rocky knoll. It is in sight of two brochs on Duirinish. The wall still stands nearly 3m high and 3.6m thick, with an internal diameter of 16.5m. The entrance is largely blocked with debris, though much remains of an intramural gallery. Below the broch there are many ancient field walls and houses of unknown age.

Dùn Gearymore (ON Garðr, G Mòr, Big Farm, NG237649, 125m) stands in a prominent position with panoramic

Dùn Gearymore

Unish House

Waternish Point, Bod an Athair and Dunvegan Head from ferry

views of the Minch and Loch Dunvegan. Although much dilapidated, the inner walls are still over 2m high. An intact intramural gallery is 8m long.

Two probable guard cells may indicate the entrance. Fragments of a scarcement layer may also be seen. The external diameter is 17m, wall thickness 3.4m, and internal diameter 11m. There are many ancient field dykes and ruined houses on the slope below. They are of unknown antiquity.

Memorial cairn

WATERNISH POINT

Park next to the graveyard, about 500m from a gate that gives access to a good track which goes all the way to Unish. After passing a large cairn, a fine view opens up along the coast. Dùn Borrafiach is about 200m east of the track on a small hillock, surrounded by field walls and remains of a large settlement.

Continue along the track to Dùn Gearymore which also overlooks old walls and ruined houses. There are fine views all around. From the ruined settlement of Bail an Tailleir the landscape changes to lush green farmland. Unish House and its surroundings are interesting to explore.

Waternish Point is about 1,000m further north. Return via the track, or for a more interesting route, follow the coastline, picking up the track at a fence shortly before the start, 9mi, 14km, 3-4h.

The Storr & Old Man reflected in the Storr Lochs, Trotternish

Trotternish - Trondairnis

Crown copyright

Trotternish (ON *Trondars Nes*, Trondar's Headland), the most northerly of Skye's peninsulas, is one of its most scenic. It also has the largest proportion of Gaelic speakers on the island, reaching nearly 50% in Kilmuir (2011 census). The Gaelic Medium Education Units at Kilmuir and Staffin Primary Schools have proven very successful and popular.

The Trotternish Ridge dominates the peninsula. It runs for nearly 15mi (24km) from Ben Dearg (NG477504, 552m) north of Portree to Sgurr Mór (NG440708, 492m) overlooking Kilmaluag in the north. The east side of the ridge is a huge escarpment with spectacular landslips. During the Palaeogene, or Tertiary Period, c.65Ma, thick flows of Basalt lava covered much older Jurassic sediments. Later, Dolerite sills penetrated weaknesses in these underlying strata.

Over time, heavily faulted underlying rocks gave way due to the weight of the stronger, denser Basalt, creating massive slumps, crumples, and pinnacles. The result is an awesome labyrinthine landscape unlike anything else in the UK. Although features such as the Old Man of Storr and the Quirang are the most famous, there are numerous other landslips in northern Skye.

Nature Trotternish has exposures of Jurassic rocks, most notably at Bearreraig, Staffin, Flodigarry, and Lub Score. Dinosaur footprints, as well as ammonites and belemnite fossils, can be seen. The area is famous for its rare alpine plants. Golden and White-tailed eagles are often seen hunting, while the rare Corncrake still breeds at Staffin. Otters are relatively common.

The Storr Lochs and the Old Man

The Storr Lochs and the Cuillin

The Quiraing from Staffin

Staffin from the Quiraing

Trotternish · Trondairnis

The Old Man of Storr and the Cuillin Ridge

THE OLD MAN OF STORR (ON *Staurr*, Stack, Rock Pillar) is one of the iconic landmarks of Skye. This 50m pinnacle points upwards like a jagged finger, slightly askew, and is visible for miles all along the east coast. The Old Man is 12m in diameter and the highest of a group of basalt spires.

Minerals, including gyrolite, apophllite, calcite, analcime, and quartz are present in the scree slopes, or can be seen eroding from the surfaces of the Basalt. The Old Man itself consists of hard, erosion resistant Gabbro. Flows of basalt of variable thicknesses and hues of red can be seen in the cliffs which tower behind. Up to thirty different layers of volcanic rocks are visible, showing how intense the eruptions were.

The Old Man and friends

The Sanctuary or *Coire Faoin* (G Lonely Corry) surrounds the Old Man and includes many other fantastically shaped spires and towers of crumbling volcanic rock, like a wild infernal version of Gaudí's *Sagrada Família* in Barcelona. Protected to the west by the towering 200m cliffs of the Storr, this place is nature at its wildest. Few of the many visitors penetrate this far.

The Storr (719m) is the highest point on the Trotternish Ridge. From its summit there are spectacular views in all directions. These include the distant Outer Hebrides, the Sound of Raasay, and the jagged Cuillin Ridge to the south.

From the top of the cliffs the desolate landscape of the Sanctuary is spread out below. To north and south the slumped and jumbled landscape is visible for miles, overlooking a relatively flat coastal plain. This in turn gives way to a coast of crumbling and rugged Basalt cliffs.

Flora This area is famous for its alpine wild flowers. These tend to grow in fissures in the Basalt, where soil has accumulated. They include Alpine and Mossy Saxifrage, Arctic Mouse-ear, Ice-

Misty day

Old Man of Storr

landic Purslane, Alpine Lady's Mantle, Mountain Sorrel, Northern Rock Cress, Globeflower, Roseroot, and Moss Campion.

Best Time to Visit The Old Man of Storr is one of the most popular walks on Skye and can get very busy at times. To avoid the crowds, and also enjoy the best lighting effects, early morning is best at all times of year. The Old Man is in the shadow of The Storr by late afternoon. In many ways, winter offers the most spectacular lighting effects.

Misty weather is ideal for a visit to the Old Man, but the Storr itself and the cliffs should be avoided except in clear conditions. Regardless of the weather or season, boots or walking shoes are essential.

Winter morning light

OLD MAN OF STORR

Parking The carpark here is often full, with vehicles extending a long way along the verges.

Walk The route starts at a gate near the carpark which then follows an excellent footpath. Towards the Old Man the way becomes much steeper with scree and loose rocks.

The whole area around the Old Man and the Sanctuary is criss-crossed by paths, making it surprisingly easy to lose the crowds, 2.5mi, 4km, 2h.

To reach the summit of the Storr, take a clear path northwards to the end of the cliffs and then up to the trig point. Either return the same way, or for a longer walk, follow the cliffs southwards to Bealach Mòr and return to the road via a path, 4mi, 6km, 4h.

BROONIE LEGEND

MacSween from Portree saved a Broonie from death, asking for no reward. Broonies are extremely ugly small creatures who are always naked and live in the sea, eating the bones of drowned seamen. They became close friends, MacSween's wife passed away suddenly due to a heart attack. Her husband then died of a broken heart.

The Broonie was very upset so he carved the Old Man of Storr in memory of his friend, and the Needle for Mrs MacSween, a deft seamstress.

Bearreraig from the viewpoint

Bearreraig (*Bjornar Vik*, Bjorni's Bay) is only 1.5mi (2km) from the often crowded Old Man of Storr, yet hardly visited. With fine coastal views, fossil packed Jurassic rocks, and a small hydro-electric power station, it is an interesting place to explore.

Storr Lochs Power Station opened in 1952 to provide electricity to Skye. It has a capacity of 2.4MW, generated from a 136m head of water. It produces an average of 8 million kWh annually. A narrow gauge railway facilitated construction and maintenance of the turbine room at the bottom of the hill.

Jurassic Fossils can be found on the foreshore here. The most famous is a species of *Ichthyosaur* which has been named *Dearcmhara shawcrossi* after Brian Shawcross, who discovered its fossilised bones here in 1959. These marine reptiles lived in shallow seas c.170 million years ago (Ma).

The best fossil beds are to the south of the bay at low tide. Belemnites are very common here, as are ammonites and bivalve molluscs. The site is an SSSI, so no hammering of fossil beds is permitted. Loose beach stones containing fossils are easily found and are continuously exposed by wave action. On no account

Intrusive volcanic rock

Belemnite fossils

should attempts to collect fossils from the cliffs be made due to the danger of rock falls.

The best time to look for fossils here is at extreme spring ebb tides after easterly gales. The shore is accessible all the way to Holm Island (c1.5mi, 2km) but it is slippery and rough going. Care should be taken to allow time to return before the tides comes back in. The shingle foreshore to the north of the burn is also good for fossil hunting. A close search of the pebbly beach at low tide offers the best opportunities. The area furthest from the burn mouth is the least visited and thus most productive.

Wildlife This quiet bay is little visited and is a good place to look for Otters. White-tailed Sea and Golden Eagles are

Volcanic boulders

Ammonite fossil

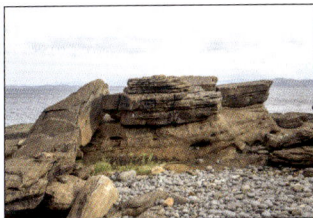
Jurassic rocks overlain with basalt

also often seen. The best strategy is to find a good viewpoint and to sit still and silently downwind of the burn mouth. Offshore, the deep waters of the Sound of Raasay sometimes harbour cetaceans.

Bearreraig Walk

Park at the end of a signposted track off the A855 at the north end of the Storr Lochs Dam.

Walk Cross the dam and take the track towards a bungalow from where a sign points to a very steep path to the power station and shore. From the top there is a dramatic view over the bay and Dolerite cliffs to the north. The steepest part has rock cut steps and a railing, but the grassy slopes can be very slippery after rain.

The shore to the south should only be explored on a falling tide to avoid getting cut off. The best fossils are found at low tide. The beach to the north can be safely accessed at any state of the tide, 2-4mi, 3-6km, 2-4h.

Trotternish east coast from Tote

The A855 north to Staffin has several very picturesque viewpoints. A section of the old road at Tote (NG521578) overlooks the Sound of Raasay. The Cuillin dominate the southern skyline, while below the 100m cliffs there is an extensive area of luxuriant greenery with many lazy beds.

Kilt Rock (NG509655) is just south of Staffin. The 55m colourful columnar Dolerite rocks, which form the cliffs, are said to resemble the tartan pleats of a kilt. There is a spectacular waterfall where nearby Loch Mealt flows into the sea. The cliffs are even grander when viewed from seaward.

Staffin Museum, in Ellishader, is across the road from the Kilt Rock viewpoint. It has displays of local fossils and minerals as well as prehistoric and more recent artefacts. Dinosaur footprint fossils are of great interest.

Loch Mealt is one of the largest expanses of freshwater on Skye. Various species of waterfowl breed here. In winter, Whooper Swans, Goldeneye and other ducks, as well as geese, are usually present. The loch margins are also of interest to botanists.

Staffin (ON *Staffr*, Rock Columns) is a thriving crofting township overlooking

Brothers' Point, Tote

Kilt Rock, Staffin

a beautiful bay. The awesome craigs of the Quiraing dominate the view to the west. The beach is famous for its fossils and dinosaur footprints. More recent inhabitants were Mesolithic people who left many artefacts in a rock shelter at An Corran, above the beach. Staffin has a well-stocked community shop.

Corncrakes This is one of the last refuges on Skye of the formerly common Corncrake. The *"crex crex"* calls of the males may still be heard in the summer, usually in the early morning or the evening. Some hay meadows are especially managed to encourage the birds.

Columba 1400 is a social enterprise based in Staffin whose purpose is *"to help young people realise that they already have the inner greatness and confidence to transform their own lives and those around them."* Since the year 2000, over 6,000 young people have benefited from their programmes. The centre has a café and library, as well as many facilities that make it invaluable to the local community and visitors.

Staffin from the south

DINOSAUR FOOTPRINTS

Staffin On the south side of the pier at Staffin an exposure of ripple-marked sandstone has about 15 dinosaur footprints. These were made by large *Ornithopods*, herbivores that walked on two legs about 165 million years ago. They are only exposed at low tide and frequently get covered in sand and seaweed. The beach here is exposed to easterly winds.

Ramha nam Brathairean (Brothers' Point NG528628) Recently a large number of dinosaur footprints have been found at this location, c.3mi (5km) south of Staffin. They were left by Saurapods and Theropods c.170Ma. There are two sets of tracks as well as many single footprints up to 0.7m in diameter. The imprints can only be seen at low tide. Access is via a track from Cul nan Cnoc. Care needs to be taken due to steep cliffs and slippery rocks.

Loch Mealt

Trotternish · Trondairnis

The Quiraing from the southwest

The Quiraing (ON *Kvi Hringr*, round cattle fold) is a place of awe and wonder where you are struck by the grandeur of nature. The eastern side of Meall na Suiramach (G *Suire*, Sea-nymph, 543m) has slumped in a vast landslip. The underlying Jurassic rocks gave way under the overlying weight of 300m thick Basalt lava.

Professor Edward Forbes put it very well, *"the truly wonderful scenery of Storr and Quiraing far surpasses for majesty any other rock landscapes in Great Britain, not excepting the Giant's Causeway."* The poet, Edwin Morgan put it more jocu-

larly, *"Tell us about last night, well, we had a wee ferintosh and we lay on the quiraing. It was pure strontian!"*

This is one of the most dramatic and wild landscapes in Britain and certainly no visit to Skye is complete without taking the short walk into the heart of these volcanic splendours. On a clear, sunny day the views are impressive, over Staffin to the Scottish mountains beyond, over the Minch to the Outer Hebrides, and south along the landslips.

The Quiraing is at its best on a misty day out of season without the crowds, when

The Quiraing is mysterious in the mist

The Table

the place takes on a dark, mysterious and eerie feeling. The fantastical rock formations seem to rise up through the gloom. It would be no surprise to meet a Hobbit, an Orc, or a dragon.

The Prison resembles a medieval fortress with its steep sides and crenellated top. The inner side is vertical rock but the south side is a grassy slope which the agile can scramble up in dry conditions.

The Needle is a striking 40m pinnacle which stands at the entrance to a mysterious world of buttresses and tumbled rocks, through which narrow paths thread their way. In this bizarre and secret world there is a feeling that an alien monster may lurk around the corner, or that it is part of a science fiction film set.

The Table is the secret heart of the Quiraing, a large flat area of grass about 100m wide, surrounded by massive ramparts. Only a few intrepid visitors penetrate this far, but the experience is essential to fully appreciate this place.

Legend says that the Trotternish farmers could hide 4,000 head of cattle here

The Needle

in times of strife. It is hard to see how even a few could be persuaded to climb up here, let alone a large herd.

THE QUIRAING

Park at the top of the escarpment on a minor road from Staffin (NG440679, 249m).

Walk The path is signposted and leads between the gaunt Prison and menacing 200m cliffs. The 40m-high Needle is one of several towering spires of rock which rear skywards. From here a twisting trail runs through gullies to the Table (3mi, 5km).

There are several ways down from here but all, except the path from the Needle, are very steep. Either return to the car on the approach route, or follow another path northwards to Fir Bhreugach, where the clifftop can be reached by a grassy slope. Keep to the path and enjoy spectacular views on the way back to the carpark (5mi, 8km, 3h).

The Prison

TROTTERNISH · TRONDAIRNIS

Duntulm Castle and the Minch

Flodigarry (N *Flyøt Garðr*, Marshy Field) is a pretty little settlement north of Staffin. Flora MacDonald and her husband lived in the cottage, which is now part of the hotel, from 1750 until 1772. Of the hotel, one guest said, *"Stunning location, fabulous food and a great nights sleep in Flora McDonald's cottage. A wonderful stay, can't wait to go back particularly for the most amazing seafood and interesting take on the menu."*

Fossils The beach here has exposures of Jurassic rocks with ammonites, belemnites and bivalves. Oxfordian and Kimmeridge clays and shales are being eroded by the sea along the shore here, revealing more fossils all the time. Park near the phone box; the boulder covered beach can be reached by several short paths.

Kendram (G *Ceann Droma*, Head of the Ridge) was the site of RAF *"Kendrom"*, Chain Home Low Radar Station 92a. The concrete structure on the hilltop protected a wooden hut which contained the radar equipment. The generator house is intact beside the road, while numerous concrete hut bases are scattered around.

The station was in operation from late 1941 until the end of 1943, when the unit was redeployed. There are extensive views over the Outer Hebrides and the Trotternish Ridge from here. The base of a Bronze Age roundhouse sits next to the 1940s structure.

Kilmaluag (G *Cille Moluag*, St. Moluag's Chapel) may well be the ancient ruined church on Port Gobhlaig in Balmaqueen. The saint was associated with the 7th century monastery in Applecross founded by St Maelruba.

Duntulm dinosaur footprint

Kilmalaug

Duntulm Castle by Wm Daniell, 1815

Rubha Hunish (ON *Hunnis Nes*, Hunni's Point) is the most northerly headland on Skye. Though low-lying itself, it is backed by 90m cliffs. It can be reached by a path which starts near the phone box, east of Duntulm. A steep ravine on the west side of Meall Tuath, 117m, leads down to the shore. This is an excellent seawatching point from which to look for migrating seabirds, whales, dolphins and Basking Sharks.

Lub Score (G *Luib*, bend; ON *Skór*, Ridge) is named from the steep escarpment facing this wide, curving bay. Huge rocks regularly tumble down the slope from the 100m basalt cliffs above.

Duntulm Castle

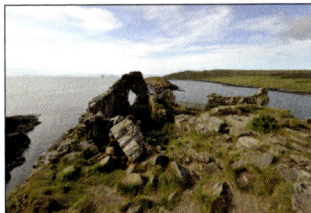

DUNTULM DINOSAURS

There are prominent fossil dinosaur footprints on the beach at Cairidh Glumaig near Duntulm Castle below the A855 (NG410739). Up to 70 cm across, they were formed by large herbivorous Sauropods in a shallow lagoon about 170 million years ago. The footprints are on a large slab of mid Jurassic Period rock which is covered at high tide.

DUNTULM CASTLE

Duntulm Castle (G *Dùn Tilm*, Castle on the Round Hillock, NG410743) is perched on a headland overlooking the Minch. Legend says that a Viking chieftain had a keep here; before that there was a broch. The ruins date from the 14th to the 17th centuries.

The MacDonalds and MacLeods fought internecine wars for centuries. In 1618 James VI granted a royal charter to Sir Donald MacDonald for Trotternish on condition that Duntulm was his seat and *"with all convenient diligence prepair materiallis and cause build ane civile and corneli house."*

It was here that a careless nurse accidentally dropped a MacDonald baby from a window. In c.1580, Uisdean MacGhilleasbuig Chlerich died a gruesome death here walled up in a dungeon after failing to kill his uncle.

Trotternish · Trondairnis

Flora MacDonald's memorial, Kilmuir

Kilmuir (G *Cille Mhuire*, Mary's Church) has a very interesting old grave-yard, with an ancient chapel and a variety of headstones. The most elaborate is that of Angus Martin with an effigy of a medieval knight. Others include an ancient Iona-style cross-head and a half-completed epitaph to Charles Mac-Arthur *"whose fame as an honest man and remarkable piper will survive this generation for his manners were easy and regular as his music and the melody of his fingers will....."*

Flora MacDonald is buried in Kilmuir graveyard. Having returned from North

Kilmuir graveyard

America in 1779, she and her husband recovered possession of the Kingsburgh estate in 1784. She died there on 4th March 1790. Over 3,000 people were said to have attended the funeral here, and between them drank 300 gallons of whisky. The memorial was put up in 1880, with the famous Samuel Johnson quotation, *"Her name will be mentioned in history and if courage and fidelity be virtues, mentioned with honour."*

Skye Museum of Island Life, opened in 1965, *"aims to preserve a township of thatched cottages, each one depicting, as closely as possible, the conditions prevailing on the island at the close of the 19th century."* The museum comprises a crofthouse, barn, weaver's cottage, smithy, and a ceilidh house. All are furnished in the manner of the time, with interesting collections of household items, tools and farm implements, as well as weaver's and blacksmith's equipment.

Kilvaxter Souterrain (G *Cille Bhagster*, The Baker's Cell NG392697) is sign-posted off the A855, south of Kilmuir. It is the storage cellar of an Iron Age house, the ruins of which stand nearby.

Museum of Island Life

The structure is lined with drystone walling and roofed by large lintels. The 17m passage is less than 75cm wide and just over 1m high. It is frequently flooded after rain.

Eilean Chalium Cille (G St Columba's Island, NG377699) is now a hillock in a large meadow, the bed of a drained loch. A small roofless chapel and an oval drystone wall are prominent. Other ruins may be the cells of a former monastery. The "island" was accessed by a substantial causeway.

Monkstadt (ON *Munki Staðir*, Monk's Farm) was originally built in the 17th century and remodelled in 1732 for Sir Alexander MacDonald of Duntulm. It was reputed to be the first house on Skye with a slate roof and was largely built using stones from Duntulm Castle. In 1798 Alexander Wentworth, 2nd Lord MacDonald, moved his seat back to Armadale.

By 1950 the house was a roofless ruin which has been beautifully restored in recent years. Nearby, *"three significant huts"* referred to by Boswell and John-

Dùn Skudiburgh

son, may be some of the monks' cells from when there was a monastery here. They are now restored complete with thatched roofs.

Kilvaxter souterrain

DÙN SKUDIBURGH

Dùn Skudiburgh (ON *Skúti Borg*, Overhanging Cliff Fort, NG373648, 61m) is an Iron Age fort dramatically situated on a large rocky outcrop. The walls of the main building are over 2m high, but hard to interpret. On the shore side there was an elaborate approach road and gateway. Nearby, the 17m Stack of Skudiburgh stands sentinel.

Walk Park in a large layby next to a quarry north of Uig on the A855 (NG385653). Follow a farm track past Skudiburgh Farm to the beach and climb up a steep hillock to explore the interesting ruins and fine views over the Minch, 3mi, 4km, 1h.

Circular Walk from Uig Follow the coast westwards to Ru Idrigill and on to Dùn Skudaburgh. Return the same way or via the first route and the road, 5mi, 8km, 2h.

Trotternish · Trondairnis

CalMac ferry leaving Uig

UIG (ON *Vik*, Bay) is one of the best natural harbours on Skye. Caledonian MacBrayne introduced the first roro car ferry to the Outer Hebrides from here in April 1964, on a triangular route to Tarbert and Lochmaddy.

Rha Waterfalls (ON *Rauðr A*, Red River) are in a beautiful small woodland which lines a steep valley. From Bridge of Rha a path climbs steeply upwards before winding through the woods to this spectacular double waterfall.

The Fairy Glen in Baile na Cnoc (G Township of the Knolls) is on a side road south of the Uig Hotel. This is a small land of fantastical knolls, mounds, and hidden places. The fairies crafted this landscape. The highest point, Castle Ewen, is easy to reach. Come on a misty winter day when there is nobody about, or early on a summer morning. There is limited parking here.

Caisteal Uisdain (G Hugh's Castle, NG380582) was built c.1580 by Hugh or, Uisdean MacGillespig Chleirich as he was known. Among his many misdemeanours he plotted to murder his uncle, Donald Gorm Mór MacDonald of Duntulm Castle. This was to be ac-

Rha Waterfalls, Uig

Fairy Glen, Uig

complished by inviting Donald Gorm for dinner, when he was to be murdered.

Unfortunately for Hugh his invitation and his instructions to the assassin were mixed up, so that his uncle learnt of his plans. Hugh soon found himself walled up in one of the dungeons at Duntulm Castle with only salt beef and an empty cup for sustenance.

Cuidrach (G Meeting Place) has an unusually sited Iron Age fort. Dùn Maraig (ON *Már Vik*, Seagull Bay) is built on a small tidal island, formerly connected by a causeway. A substantial wall defends the west side of the islet. There are several ruined buildings visible.

Kensalayre (G *Ceann*, Head; ON *Eyre*, Gravel Beach) is at the head of Loch Eyre. The Sornaichean Coir' Fhinn (G *Sorn*, Kiln NG414525) Standing Stones here are both nearly 1m high and stand just above the shore. Here, Fhinn roasted whole deer in a giant pot set on three stones, one of which has disappeared. Nearby there are several large Neolithic chambered cairns.

Kensalayre Standing Stones

Clach Ard Pictish Stone (G Tall Stone) stands in the township of Tote (ON *Topt*, Homestead, NG421491), near the estuary of the River Snizort. This 1.4m basalt pillar was used as a door jamb in a nearby house until c.1880, when it was re-erected here. It is now protected by a rather mean looking fence .

This is a Class I Pictish symbol stone, dating from the 7th century, one of only four found on Skye and Raasay. There is a *crescent and V-rod* at the top, followed by *double disc and Z-rod*, with a *mirror and comb* at the bottom, all of which are commonly-occurring symbols.

Caisteal Uisdean, Cuidrach

CAISTEAL UISDEAN

Walk From the Cuidrach side road (NG378596) take a track southwards and then along the coast to Caisteal Uisdain. The castle is built on the edge of a low cliff and measures 15m by 10m externally. The walls are about 5m high. It can be entered by a narrow window.

Raasay - Ratharsair

Crown copyright

The Narrows of Raasay from the Moll road

RAASAY (ON *Ra Ass Ey*, Roe Deer Ridge Island) lies between Skye and Applecross on the Scottish mainland. It covers 6,231ha, is 14mi (23km) long and 3mi (5km) wide. Its varied geology results in a variety of terrain. The south end has granite on the west. Heavily faulted Jurassic sandstone, shale, and limestone outcrop here also.

Beds of Oolitic Ironstone, a type of limestone, inland from Inverarish, were commercially exploited during WWI. At the north end underlying Torridonian Sandstone gives to ancient Lewisian Gneiss, creating the rough landscape of the Arnish peninsula and Rona.

During the Norse period Raasay belonged to the Bishopric of the Isles. After the Treaty of Perth in 1266, it came under the Earldom of Ross. Traditionally, the island was held by the MacSweens, a Norse/Gaelic family, but by the early 16th century the MacLeods of Lewis had taken over.

MV Hallaig at Sconser

Balachuirn house

Clachan from the ferry pier

The island enjoyed something of a golden age under succeeding MacLeod chieftains, until the 13th chief, John MacLeod was bankrupted in 1843. From then until 1911, when it was bought by William Baird & Co of Coatbridge, Raasay had a series of increasingly unpleasant owners. Finally, in 1923, the Board of Agriculture for Scotland bought the island and started to resettle crofts.

BUTEC Inner Sound and the Sound of Raasay are both very deep, scoured out by huge glaciers during the Ice Age. Inner Sound is over 200m deep in places and is used as a submarine exercise and weapons testing area. The British Underwater Test and Evaluation Centre (BUTEC) Range covers the deepest part. Its base is in Kyle of Lochalsh.

Population Most of the population of 161 (2011 census) live in the southeast of the island. Unlike on Skye where the number of residents has started to rise, the population here continued to decline between 2001 and 2011. The Clearances of the 19th century destroyed whole communities. Today Raasay is developing its own brand of tourism.

MV "Hallaig"

MV *"Hallaig"*, which began service on the route from Sconser on Skye to Raasay in October 2013, is an innovative hybrid diesel-electric vessel. Built at a cost of £10m, this 43.5m ferry is powered by a combination of three Volvo Penta diesels and a large bank of lithium ion batteries which drive two 375kW electric motors. The batteries are recharged overnight at the pier, and provide 20% of the power. The vessel can carry 150 passengers plus 23 cars or 2 HGVs. She has a service speed of 9 knots. When under battery power she is virtually silent.

Raasay - Ratharsair

Clachan is the main settlement

Clachan (G Hamlet) is the arrival point for the ferry from Sconser in Skye. The crossing takes 25 minutes, affording fine views of the Red Hills, Inner Sound and the Trotternish Ridge. Many of the sites of interest are within a short walk of the ferry terminal. Raasay has a large network of footpaths, tracks, and minor roads which make it a delight to explore on foot or by bicycle.

Raasay House originally dates from the 15th century and was rebuilt in 1720. It was burned down in 1746 by government soldiers who ransacked the island. Malcolm MacLeod had supported the Jacobites and helped Bonnie Prince Charlie to escape. It was rebuilt soon after and later extended by the next chief, who so lavishly entertained Boswell and Johnson in 1773.

The house was further developed during the 19th century. After a succession of owners and neglect, it was finally bought by the Raasay House Community Company in 2007. After major renovations and a disastrous fire it reopened in 2013. It offers hotel and hostel accommodation, a restaurant, café and bar, as well as a wide range of outdoor activities.

Kilmaluag (G *Cille Moluag*, St. Moluag's Chapel), the former parish church, dates

Napoleonic battery and mermaid

Raasay House

from the late 12th or early 13th century. St Maelrubha established a sanctuary in the late 6th century, surrounded by eight carved symbol stones, of which only one now survives. An 11th century chapel with a fine carved stone doorway and lintel stands near the gate.

A Pictish Stone (NG547368) stands inside a metal gate off the road 100m north of Raasay House. It was re-erected here in the 19th century after being dug up by road men. This Class I stone has *tuning fork* and *crescent with Z-rod* symbols. Above them a contemporary *Chi-Rho* cross is also incised, perhaps on top of a *mirror symbol*.

There is a similar incised-cross on a granite slab on the east face of the Battery (NG546363). Both crosses and the symbols may be from the 6th century. They are thought to be two of the sanctuary markers erected by St Maelrubha.

The Battery was built in 1809 during the Napoleonic Wars, to defend the Narrows of Raasay. It mounted six cannon. It is still protected by two large breasted mermaids who watch over the operations of the ferry.

Home Farm is a model steading, built in 1795-1805. Its buildings include byres, stables, workshops, a dairy, and a tack room, surrounding a central court. The clock stopped working in 1914 when thirty-six Raasaymen marched off to war, only fourteen came back.

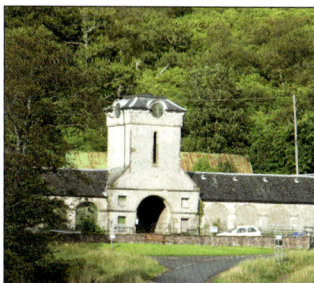

Home Farm, Clachan

Souterrain A large Iron Age souterrain, *Uamh nan Ramh* (G Oar Cave) was built by roofing over a cleft in the rocks with wide lintels. The passage is at least 16m long, 0.9m wide and 1.1m high at the entrance. It is near the old jetty.

Dùn Borodale (NG553364, 91m) is an unusual oval broch situated on a small hill in Borodale Wood. The south side stands over 2.5m high. The entrance passage is full of tumbled rubble. There is an intramural gallery, a scarcement layer, and a doorway to a probable blocked-up stairway. The surrounding trees were cut down, revealing its strategic position.

Raasay House in 1815 by William Daniell

Raasay - Ratharsair

Inverarish iron mine and conifer plantation

Inverarish (G *Inver*, N *Aros Nes*, Burn-mouth Point) is a curious hybrid Gaelic/Norse name, like many on Skye. Most of the village was developed during 1911-1915 by William Baird & Co of Coatbridge to accommodate workers in its nearby iron mine. With a shop, Post Office, and its pretty terraced cottages, Inverarish is the main settlement on Raasay.

Watermill An interesting 18th century watermill sits abandoned near the burn mouth. It has interesting stonework, perhaps derived from the original Raasay House. A carved stone dated 1720

with the initials of Malcolm Macleod and Mary Mackenzie may celebrate their newly rebuilt home.

WWI Iron Mine The remains of the Baird & Co mine workings are in woodland northeast of the village (NG565365). The tunnels cannot be visited but the entrances and associated roofless buildings may be seen. The remains of a light railway, which carried raw ore 1.5mi (2.5km) down to the processing works, associated facilities, and the concrete pier at Suisinish, can all be seen.

Woodland According to legend, much of Raasay was formerly wooded. From the 18th century the precincts of Raasay House were planted with trees. In 1949 the Forestry Commission started large scale forestry in the area northeast of Clachan and Inverarish, taking in the former mining works. Inverarish Forest has a variety of waymarked paths.

Raasay Stores

WWI iron mine with German POWs

Suisinish (ON *Seyis Nes*, Seething Point) lies to the south of the village, facing the Narrows of Raasay with their strong tidal streams; hence the name. The south road ends at Eyre Point, where there are some remains of a Neo-lithic chambered cairn.

Fearns (G *Fearna*, Alder) is the only remaining settlement on the east coast. Patches of ancient woodland, mostly Birch, Alder, Ash, Hazel, and Oak, survive along the coast here. This whole area was brutally cleared by George Rainy from 1843 in favour of sheep. Later, Red Deer were encouraged as "sporting" became popular with the wealthy.

Hallaig (ON *Hallr Vik*, slope bay, NG591385) is the subject of a beautiful and poignant poem by Sorley MacLean, who was born on Raasay. At the time of the Clearance here in 1854, Hallaig may have been the biggest settlement on Raasay. The remains of over forty houses, dykes, fields, and outhouses can be explored. The large sheep fank was built using stones from the houses.

Sheltered by the cliffs of Dùn Caan, and situated on fertile Jurassic limestone and calcareous sandstone, this is the most fertile part of the island. Before the Clearances, a thriving agricultural community prospered here for thousands of years. Plenty of time should be allowed to explore the ruins, ancient areas of woodland, and dramatic scenery.

Eyre Point, Suisnish

Fossils The extensive exposures of Jurassic sediments on southeast Raasay are well exposed in the Hallaig area. Heavy faulting means a great variety of limestones, shales, sandstones, and clays may be seen in a relatively small area.

Boulders and broken rocks on the shoreline, especially at low tide, or below inland cliffs, are good places to start looking. Stream beds and burn mouths may turn up fossils washed out of inland beds. Ammonites, belemnites, a variety of scallops, and other bivalves as well as gastropods may be found here.

HALLAIG

Walk Park at the end of the public road from Inverarish at Fearns (NG593359). A sign indicates the grassy track which goes northwards to Hallaig. About halfway to the ruined village there is a memorial cairn to Sorley Maclean. His poem *"Hallaig"* is inscribed on a plaque here in Gaelic and English; 4mi, 6km, 2-3h, but all day if fossil hunting.

Raasay - Ratharsair

Dùn Caan and Loch na Meilich

Oskaig (ON *Oss Vik*, Sandbank Bay) is a pretty group of houses just north of Clachan. It was here that the famous Gaelic poet, Sorley Maclean, was born in 1911.

Skye and mist from Dùn Caan
Dùn Caan and Raasay from Braes

Dùn Caan (G *Dùn* ON *Knut*, Canute's Hill, 443m) is the highest point on Raasay. Its prominent "Dutch Cap" is formed by an intrusive lava flow of Olivine Basalt. Several extensive dykes run across this area. The east side of the summit has precipitous cliffs and offers panoramic views on a clear day. When Boswell visited here in 1773 he danced a jig of delight at the vista he beheld. The shortest route starts from a layby, just south of Balmeanach (NG561406).

Calum's Road was built by Calum MacLeod, of Arnish, (ON *Erne Nes*, Sea-
Calum's Road

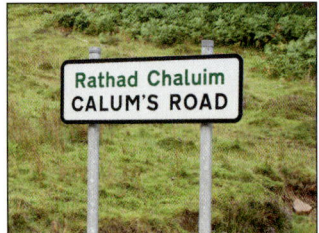

Brochel Castle

Brochel Castle in 1815 by William Daniell

eagle Point) in 1964-1974. He used his strength, a manual on road making, a pick, a shovel, and a wheelbarrow. The road runs for 1.75mi (2.8km) north from Brochel Castle. It was adopted and surfaced by Highlands Council in 1972. A memorial cairn commemorates his achievement.

Rona (ON *Hraun-ey*, Rocky Island), just north of Raasay, is low-lying and formed of ancient Lewisian Gneiss. Only two people currently live on the island now, managing the island for a Danish company. This is perhaps the most remote B&B and self-catering accommodation in the Inner Hebrides. Rona can be reached by chartering a boat from Portree.

Calum's Road hut

Brochel Castle

Brochel Castle (ON *Borg*, fort, NG584462) is in the northeast of Raasay, on a 15m Torridonian conglomerate stack. Surrounded by lush green grassland, due to underlying Jurassic sediments, it is the most dramatic and romantic of Skye's castles.

There may have been a broch and then a Norse keep on this strategically situated rock. The Vikings were probably MacSweens, descended from Swein Alsleifson, of the *Orkneyinga Saga*.

The first records date from the 15th century, when the Lewis MacLeods were supreme in the region. They controlled Gairloch and the Coigach, but were beaten by constant conflict. In c.1671 the family seat moved to the more congenial area of Clachan.

Much of the castle has collapsed since Daniell's visit in 1815, but the former splendour of this ruin can still be imagined. The slopes are strewn with the remains of a substantial settlement, including an ancient chapel. Over 400 people lived here in 1912.

GETTING TO SKYE

ISLE OF SKYE
GO NORTH THIS YEAR
BRITISH RAILWAYS   TRAVEL BY RAIL

By Road to Portree			
Departure	mi	km	time
London	624	1004	11:30
Dover	710	1143	12:30
Stranraer	297	478	6:40
Edinburgh	235	378	5:00
Aberdeen	216	348	5:00
Inverness	113	182	2:30
Scrabster	203	327	4:30
Ullapool	119	192	2:30

Rail - Kyle Line			
Inverness	80	129	2:37
Glasgow - Kyle of Lochalsh			6:28
London - Kyle of Lochalsh			11:31
Rail - West Highland Line			
Fort William	84	135	1:21
Glasgow - Mallaig			5:14
London - Mallaig			11:05

THE ISLE OF SKYE has been a popular visitor destination for nearly 200 years, ever since the introduction of regular steamer services and the development of public roads. The island is directly reached via the Skye Bridge as well as by ferries from Mallaig, Glenelg, Tarbert in Harris, and Lochmaddy in North Uist; making it the most accessible island in Scotland.

Road When the Skye Bridge opened in 1995, travel to the island was transformed overnight. This is but one of several ways of getting to the Isle of Skye, all of which involve traversing spectacular and remote landscapes.

There are two main approaches. From the south, the A82 runs from Glasgow to Fort William; the same road follows Loch Ness to Inverness. The A86 connects with the A9 at Dalwhinnie. From Fort William, the picturesque A830 to Mallaig winds for 43mi (67km) past Glenfinnan, Loch Morar, and Arisaig.

From Dingwall, north of Inverness, the A832 and A890 connect with the A87 east of Kyle, the main route into Kyle of Lochalsh from the Great Glen. It connects with the A82 at Invergarry. All these routes can be slow going when busy or in poor weather conditions. lochalsh.co.uk

One of the most spectacular routes to Skye is via Glenelg. From Shiel Bridge at the head of Loch Duich a narrow side road winds its way up and over the Bealach Ratagan (348m), to the remote valley of Glenelg with its Iron Age brochs, 18th century barracks, and old fashioned car ferry.
skyeferry.co.uk

Rail The railway links to Skye are also extremely picturesque. They traverse areas of high natural scenic beauty as they wind at a leisurely pace to Kyle of Lochalsh and Mallaig. The Kyle Line runs from Dingwall to Kyle of Lochalsh, passing through remote countryside. The coastal section from Lochcarron to Plockton is particularly splendid.
scotrail.co.uk

The West Highland Line from Fort William to Mallaig may be the most romantic way to travel to Skye, especially when a steam locomotive is providing the traction. The Caledonian Sleeper from London Euston to Fort William can be combined with the train to Mallaig. From here a ferry runs to Armadale, where a hire car can be picked up.
sleeper.scot

The *Jacobite* steam hauled train runs from May until October along the West Highland line from Fort William to Mallaig. British Railways called it *"A Line for All Seasons"*. It is one of the most scenic railway journeys in the world, with the iconic curved Glenfin-

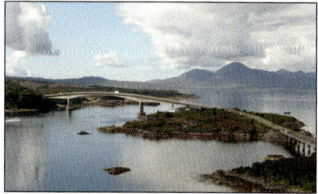
Skye Bridge from Plock of Kyle

nan viaduct and its twenty one tall arches. It features in many films, including the Harry Potter series.
westcoastrailways.co.uk

Ferries link Skye to the Scottish mainland from Mallaig and Glenelg. The Mallaig to Armadale route is convenient for those driving from the south or travelling by train. The Glenelg to Kylerhea service is operated by a small turntable boat, like the original 1934 version.

Outer Hebrides Ferries Uig in Trotternish, 15 miles north of Portree, is the ferry port for Tarbert on the Isle of Harris and Lochmaddy on The North Uist. A variety of circular tours of the Outer Hebrides are possible by means of other ferries to Ullapool and Oban.
calmac.co.uk

Portree and steamship in the late 1800s

GETTING TO & AROUND IN SKYE

MV Hallaig at Sconser Pier

Airport Although there is a small airfield near Broadford, there are no scheduled flights into Skye. The facility is used by private and charter aircraft, as well as the air ambulance.

Buses to Skye Citylink *"offers the perfect way to travel to Skye. From Glasgow there are three direct services a day and a fourth to Fort William. If you are travelling from Edinburgh you can reach Skye by connecting in Glasgow on Service 900 or by travelling as far as Fort William on Service 913, which runs daily during the summer season between May and October."*
citylink.co.uk

Travel within Skye involves considerable distances, mostly on excellent modern roads. Many of the side roads are single track with passing places which

CalMac ferry at Uig Pier

must be used to allow vehicles to pass each other. The table opposite provides distances in miles between some of the main centres.

Car Parking remains free in most of Skye except for the centre of Portree. Charges are now being introduced to finance local infrastructure such as at the Fairy Pools.

Buses within Skye are operated by Stagecoach who have good daily services to the main settlements during the week. The timetable is limited at weekends. stagecoachbus.com

Taxis are a useful option for transport on Skye, especially when planning long linear walks. They are also a good choice (but expensive) for those not wishing to drive. There are taxi companies in Portree, Kyle of Lochalsh, Dunvegan, and elsewhere. Half or full day tours are good value.

Car Hire Several companies offer car hire on the Isle of Skye. This is a strongly recommended option for those arriving by air or train as it offers complete flexibility whilst touring the island. Those arriving by air in Inverness, Edinburgh, or Glasgow should also consider car hire on arrival.
jans.co.uk

Cycling is a delight on the Isle of Skye. Despite the high mountains, most of the terrain is not hilly. Apart from the main road from the Skye Bridge to Portree, most of the roads are quiet except in the peak holiday season. Bicycles may also be hired or repaired in Portree. The distances will be of no concern for those used to cycling, but may prove challenging for the unfit.

Boat Trips are run from Portree, Elgol, Stein, Uig, Staffin, and Dunvegan. Several operators offer excursions from Portree to see White-tailed Sea Eagles and other wildlife. Elgol is the departure point for Loch Coruisk at the heart of the Cuillins, and for wildlife cruises.

Guided Tours range from sedate walks or minibus tours to the epic and challenging Cuillin Ridge traverse. A range of operators are available here. A selection are listed in the information pages. Guided walks are particularly popular.

Portree Harbour with tour boats

Cruise Ships Portree and Dunvegan are increasingly on the itinerary of the smaller ships which cruise the Hebrides. Passengers are disembarked via tenders to pontoons at the dockside. Excursions from Portree include Dunvegan Castle, Talisker Distillery, Skye Museum of Island Life, the Clan Donald Centre, and the Trotternish Peninsula.

Skye Distances in Miles	Skye Bridge	Portree	Armadale	Broadford	Dunvegan	Elgol	Glen Brittle	Neist Point	Sligachan	Staffin	Uig
Skye Bridge	0	33	21	8	47	22	35	56	24	50	47
Portree	33	0	40	24	21	38	24	30	9	17	15
Armadale	21	40	0	16	54	30	47	66	31	58	57
Broadford	8	24	16	0	38	14	31	49	15	42	41
Dunvegan	47	21	54	38	0	52	27	11	23	38	27
Elgol	22	38	30	14	52	0	45	63	29	56	54
Glen Brittle	35	35	47	31	27	52	0	37	16	38	39
Neist Point	56	30	66	49	11	62	37	0	32	49	39
Sligachan	24	9	31	15	23	29	16	32	0	26	25
Staffin	50	17	58	42	38	56	38	49	26	0	10
Uig	47	15	57	41	27	54	39	39	25	10	0

Intinerary #1 - A (Long) Day in Skye

copyright Helen Stirling Maps

The Isle of Skye is probably the most scenic place in Scotland, easily accessible over the Skye Bridge or by ferry. A visit can take the whole day in summer but really the island needs much longer. Here are some suggestions for a very full day's visit.

The main sites are obvious and can be very busy during the day, but quiet in early morning or the evening. There are a vast number of places to visit which are not far from the tourist route that are beautiful and delightful to visit after a short walk.

WHAT TO SEE & DO

A (LONG) DAY IN SKYE

1. Eilean Donan Castle is in a spectacular position on a small tidal island where Loch Alsh, Loch Duich and Loch Long meet at Dornie. The Castle and Visitor Centre are open most of the year.

Kyle of Lochalsh is the terminus of the picturesque Kyle Line from Inverness. This busy village has interesting shops and places to stay and boat trips.

The Skye Bridge (p12) is a graceful curve from Kyle to Kyleakin. The best views are gained by walking or cycling. The viewpoint at Ploc of Kyle offers a dramatic panoramic view of Skye.

Kyleakin is bypassed by the bridge, but it remains a good centre to explore southern Skye and Lochalsh.

2. Broadford (p13) is a strip of houses, hotels, and shops strung out along the A850 around Broadford Bay.

7. Sligachan (p42) is at the crossroads of the roads to Portree and Dunvegan. The view to the Cuillin over the old Telford bridge is one of the most iconic on the Isle of Skye. It is at its most spectacular when the river is in spate, when a low sun comes out after a deluge.

8. Talisker Distillery (p49) is in Carbost. Tours are run except during the quiet season. The Talisker Tasting Tour is recommended.

The Oyster Shed (p48) is up a steep lane above Talisker Distillery. This eclectic and unique shop cum takeaway is not to be missed by lovers of seafood. There are cracking views too.

9. The Fairy Pools (p46) at the head of Glen Brittle are at their most impressive after heavy rain, although access may be difficult. They are best visited outside of busy periods. There is a large car park with toilets (payment fee).

10. Portree (p54) The main settlement in Skye faces east and is very sheltered. Quay Street has a row of brightly painted houses, while Beaumont Crescent curves elegantly around.

12. Dunvegan Castle (p70) is said to be the oldest occupied house in Scotland; it exudes history and romance. The gardens are well worth a visit.

13. Neist Point (p80) is one of the most visited places on Skye. Many come to see sunsets over the Outer Hebrides. Loch Mór, on the approach to Neist Point, makes a perfect foreground.

16. Old Man of Storr (p94) is 6mi (10km) north of Portree on the A855. The walk to this 50m pinnacle and the Sanctuary is one of the most popular on Skye and parking may be difficult. The best times to go are early morning, or evening. (2.5mi, 4km, 2h return).

The Storr (p94, 719m) is reached by an easy path north from the Old Man, panoramic views (4mi, 6km, 4h return).

17. The Quiraing (p100) is signposted north of Staffin. This place of wonder has huge landslips and a labyrinth of fantastical rock formations. Access is via a path from the carpark at the top of the ridge (3mi, 5km, 2h).

Intinerary #2 - North Skye

copyright Helen Stirling Maps

North Skye is scenically spectacular. The Duirinish, Waternish, and Trotternish peninsulas are all different and yet dramatic. Apart from the key sites of Dunvegan Castle, Neist Point, the Quiraing, and the Storr there are many lesser visited places.

The Cuillin Ridge is prominent on the southern horizon from many places. Volcanic rocks form most of Duirinish, Waternish, and Trotternish. The collapsing strata of the Trotternish ridge are especially spectacular at the Storr and the Quiraing.

A Day in North Skye

10. Portree (p54) The main settlement on Skye faces east and is very sheltered. Quay Street lines the pier with a row of brightly painted houses, while Beaumont Crescent curves elegantly around.

11. Cuillin Viewpoints (p42) The Cuillin Ridge is prominent to the south all along the road here and to Portree.

Bracadale (p60) is approached from the east via the steep Amar River ravine. This area has many ancient monuments.

Gesto (p61) was farmed by MacLeods for centuries. This sheltered bay is one of the prettiest on the whole island.

12. Dunvegan Castle (p70) The oldest occupied house in Scotland exudes history and romance, excellent gardens.

The Coral Beaches (p73) at Claigan are 3.5mi (5km) north of Dunvegan Castle. The beaches here are perhaps the finest on Skye and are formed from maerl and seashells (2.5mi, 4km, 1-3h).

13. Neist Point (p80) is one of the most visited places on Skye. Many come to see sunsets over the Outer Hebrides. Loch Mór, on the approach to Neist Point, makes a perfect foreground.

14. Waternish (p84) The Fairy Bridge is the subject of many legends; the best time to visit is on a misty, moonlit night.

Stein (p84) Built by the British Fisheries Society in the late 18th century but was never a successful fishing station.

Trumpan Church (p86) burnt by the MacDonalds in 1578 resulting in the Battle of the Spoiling of the Dyke.

16. Old Man of Storr (p94) is 6mi (10km) north of Portree on the A855. The walk to this 50m pinnacle and the Sanctuary is one of the most popular on Skye and parking may be difficult. The best times to go are early morning, or evening. (2.5mi, 4km, 2h return).

The Storr (p94, 719m) is reached by an easy path north from the Old Man, panoramic views (4mi, 6km, 4h return).

17. The Quiraing (p100) is signposted north of Staffin. This place of wonder has huge landslips and a labyrinth of fantastical rock formations. Access is via a path from the carpark at the top of the ridge (3mi, 5km, 2h).

18. Duntulm Castle (p103) is ruinous, the seat of the MacDonalds for 200 years before moving to Monkstadt.

Dinosaur Tracks (p103) are on a slab of rock exposed at low tide at the east end of Lub Score, near Duntulm Castle.

Rubha Hunish (p103) The most northerly on Skye is good for seawatching.

Flora MacDonald (p104) is buried in the Kilmuir graveyard. There are a number of much older graveslabs.

The Museum of Island Life (p104) opposite the graveyard is a group of buildings dating from the late 19th century.

19. Uig (p106) is attractively sited around a sheltered bay. With a brewery, hotel, shops and a filling station, this ferry port is a good base for touring.

The Fairy Glen (p106) A fantastical land, best on a misty day.

Rha Waterfalls (p106) cascade over a drop in woods near Rha Bridge in Uig.

Intinerary#3 - South Skye

copyright Helen Stirling Maps

Southern Skye is much gentler than the north. Sleat, Strathaird and Elgol all offer spectacular scenery. The fertile land here once supported a large population and many cattle. Fishing was a big part of the economy. Ancient woodlands survive here too.

The limestone areas in Starthaird support a vast range of plants. Blaven is an outlier of the Cuillin, and Loch Curuisk in the heart of the Cuillin is especially recommended. Elgol and Camasunary are equally lovely places to visit.

A DAY IN SOUTHERN SKYE

2. Broadford (p13) is a strip of houses, hotels and shops. Access to the peninsulas of Sleat and Strathaird from here.

3. Isle Ornsay (p21) is named after the tidal island that shelters its stone built harbour. It has a romantic old inn, an art gallery and a fashion boutique.

Ord (p23) is attractively sited on Loch Eishort facing Strathaird and the Cuillin. There are several areas of ancient woodland in this area with rare lichens and mosses.

Tokavaig (p23) is above a pretty bay with spectacular views to the Cuillin.

Dunscaich Castle (p23) stands on a rock about 500m from the road. It was abandoned in c.1539 after a long and bloody history of dreadful deeds.

Tarskavaig (p23) overlooks a fine cove with impressive views over the Cuillin.

4. Sabhal Mòr Ostaig (p24) "This College is a National Centre for Gaelic Language and Culture and there are lots of learning opportunities for people with an interest in Gaelic." It was founded by Sir Ian Noble in 1973.

Knock Castle (p24) is on a headland in Knock Bay. This romantic ruin was abandoned in c.1690. It was an important MacDonald stronghold.

Armadale (p25) has been a ferry port since the early 1800s.

Clan Donald Centre (p25) and the Museum of the Isles tells the story of Clan Donald. It has shops and a café.

Ardvasar (p25) is the largest settlement on Sleat, the inn established in 1812.

5. Strathaird (p28) the A881 from Broadford to Elgol is a single track road which passes through some of Skye's most beautiful and dramatic areas.

Strath Suardal (p28) is a verdant green valley, overlooked by Beinn na Caillich. The Durness Limestone here is home to plants which prefer calcareous soils.

Cille Chriosd (p29) is a roofless 16th century church surrounded by an ancient graveyard. This now deserted glen once supported a vibrant community.

Torrin (p30) is a pretty settlement with colourful gardens, lush fields of grass, and the only marble quarry in the UK. The Blue Shed Café is recommended for its views, cakes, and coffee.

Camas Malag (p30) is reached by a side road. The beach is characterised by pebbles. Splendid views across Loch Slapin to Blaven and Beinn na Caillich. Suisnish and Boreraig were cleared in the 1850s. A track goes from Camas Malag. A fine circular walk, returning by a moorland path (10mi, 16km, 3h).

6. Camasunary (p35) is reached by a track which starts south of Kilmarie (2.5mi, 4km, 2h) or by a coastal walk from Elgol (8mi, 6km, 3h return).

Elgol (p36) is an enchanting place. The views over Loch Scavaig to the Cuillin Ridge are divine in every season.

Loch Coruisk (p38) Boat trips run from Elgol to this dramatic glacial valley in the heart of the Cuillin. A visit is one of the unmissable highlights of a visit to Skye (circuit 5mi, 8km, 4h).

BIBLIOGRAPHY

CHARLES TAIT GUIDE BOOKS

The Isle of Skye Guide Book	Charles Tait	Charles Tait Photo	2020
The Orkney Guide Book, 5th ed	Charles Tait	Charles Tait Photo	2021
Heart of Neolithic Orkney, 2nd ed	Charles Tait	Charles Tait Photo	2018
The Orkney Peedie Guide, 5th ed	Charles Tait	Charles Tait Photo	2019
The Shetland Guide Book	Charles Tait	Charles Tait Photo	2019
The Outer Hebrides Guide Book	Charles Tait	Charles Tait Photo	2019
The NC500 Guide Book	Charles Tait	Charles Tait Photo	2021

LOCAL BOOKS

Skye, The Island and its Legends	Otta Swire	Birlinn	2006
Western Seaboard Illus Arch Guide	Mary Miers	Rutland Press	2008
Skye	Derek Cooper	Routledge	1969
A Description of the Western Isles	Martin Martin	Birlinn	1698
An Island Odyssey	Hamish Haswell-Smith	Canongate	1999

NATURE BOOKS

Collins Bird Guide	Mullarney et al	HarperCollins	2000
Butterflies & Moths	Sterry & Mackay	Dorling Kindersley	2004
Wild Flowers of Britain	Blamey, Fitter & Fitter	A&C Black	2003
Skye Birds	RL McMillan	skye-birds.com	2009
Skye, Landscape Geology	Stephenson & Merritt	SNH	2006
The Botanist in Skye	Murray & Binks	Murray & Binks	2005

WALKING - ISLE OF SKYE

Isle of Skye Natural History Walks	Chris Mitchell	Sigma Press	2010
Isle of Skye Rambler's Guide	Chris Townsend	Collins	2001
Walking the Isle of Skye	Terry Marsh	Cicerone	2015

ORDNANCE SURVEY MAPS

OS Explorer Map 407	Skye - Dunvegan	Ordnance Survey	2020
OS Explorer Map 408	Skye – Trotternish & Storr	Ordnance Survey	2020
OS Explorer Map 409	Raasay, Rona & Scalpay	Ordnance Survey	2020
OS Explorer Map 410	Portree & Bracadale	Ordnance Survey	2020
OS Explorer Map 411	Skye – Cuillin Hills	Ordnance Survey	2020
OS Explorer Map 412	Skye - Sleat	Ordnance Survey	2020
OS Landranger Map 23	North Skye	Ordnance Survey	2020
OS Landranger Map 24	Raasay & Applecross	Ordnance Survey	2020
OS Landranger Map 32	South Skye & Cuillin Hills	Ordnance Survey	2020
OS Landranger Map 33	Loch Alsh, Glen Shiel	Ordnance Survey	2020

INDEX

Some Suggested Places to Visit